ARE THE JEWS A RACE?

Are the Jews a Race?
by Karl Kautsky — Translated
from the 2nd German edition

GREENWOOD PRESS, PUBLISHERS
WESTPORT, CONNECTICUT

The Library of Congress has catalogued this publication as follows:

Library of Congress Cataloging in Publication Data

Kautsky, Karl, 1854–1938.
  Are the Jews a race?

  Translation of Rasse und judentum.
  1. Jews. I. Title.
GN547.K3813 1972   572.8'924   75–97288
ISBN 0–8371–2611–8

Originally published in 1926 by International Publishers Co.,
Inc., New York

Reprinted in 1972 by Greenwood Press, Inc.,
51 Riverside Avenue, Westport, Conn. 06880

Library of Congress catalog card number 75-97288

ISBN 0-8371-2611-8

Printed in the United States of America

10 9 8 7 6 5 4 3 2

PUBLISHER'S NOTE

Are the Jews a Race now appears for the first time in English. The first German edition appeared in 1914, under the title *Rasse und Judentum*; the second edition, in 1921, already included a number of important additions and improvements, particularly the new chapter entitled "Zionism After the War"; for the present English version, the author has revised and brought up to date the second German edition, in the light of recent developments in Palestine.

CONTENTS

ARE THE JEWS A RACE?

ARE THE JEWS A RACE?

CHAPTER I

RACE THEORIES

"On the Jew's *faith* I do not look, his *race* is what I cannot brook",[1] is the motto of modern anti-Semitism, which—contrary to the naïve anti-Semitism of earlier periods—is proud of its scientific spirit and feels itself free from religious prejudices. Just as religion was once obliged, and is still obliged, to cloak or justify all possible varieties of secular partisan interests, so natural science must now aid in representing aspirations of interests with strictly temporal and spacial limitations as natural and eternal necessities.

This does not mean that religion formerly—and the natural sciences now—were actually created for such purposes by interested parties, as is sometimes maintained with regard to religion. Both grow from entirely different roots. But as soon as either has become a force dominating the thought of men, each social stratum finds itself impelled to make use of this force and to justify its interests on

[1] *Was der Jude glaubt, ist einerlei,*
In der Rasse liegt die Schweinerei.

11

the basis of this force. When, at the end of the Eleventh Century, the nations of western and central Europe had been relieved of the pressure of the Slavs and Arabs to such an extent as to enable them to take the offensive and plunder the wealthy Orient, they inaugurated their predatory campaigns—the Crusades—with the battle-cry: *Dieu le veult!* And when, a few centuries later, after the Turks had again pushed back the Christians in the Mediterranean, and the rising capitalism of western Europe was crying for colonial booty and finding ready tools for its adventurous expeditions to new continents in the declining knighthood and the expropriated peasants, these continents were visited with fire and sword, plunder and serfdom, in order to bring the light of true religion to the heathen for the greater glory of God. And the class struggles in Europe itself, which were then disintegrating feudalism and ushering in capitalism, were conducted as late as in the Seventeenth Century by the various parties with constant invocations of the Bible and the Fathers of the Church. Since then religion has lost its power. As industrial capitalism advances, the religious mode of thought is replaced by the scientific mode of thought. Religion still maintains itself for a period, by force of habit, as a conservative power, but the motive springs of the ensuing social evolution cease to make use of religious modes of thought and arguments. The advances of the new, capitalist mode of production are closely connected with the advances in the natural sciences. Each serves as a powerful stimulus to the other. The bourgeois intelligentsia now demand that all social aspirations be in accord with natural science, *i.e.*, with the recognized laws of nature; each social interest must find its justification in its compatibility with the laws of nature. In this connection, however, human society sometimes still fails to be regarded as a specific portion of nature, having its own laws, just as organic nature has its own laws as distinguished from those of inorganic nature. The inadequacy of this point of view easily becomes apparent, producing a reaction in favour of isolating human society, or man himself, as a social, ethical creature, from the natural laws of causality. The bourgeois philosophy of our times moves between these two extremes.

Once Darwinism had completed its victorious procession through the natural sciences, it was regarded as up-to-date to apply it without further ado to social conditions also. There are no sudden leaps in nature, but only imperceptible transformations, therefore natural science forbids revolution as a violation of natural laws. The struggle for existence is represented as an eternal process, wherefor it is contrary to nature to construct a society without competition, etc.

In the last few decades it is particularly the conception of *race* that enjoys precedence as an explanation, or rather justification, of social institutions and aspirations.

A colonial policy is represented by the theoreticians of race as a natural necessity, as a consequence of the fact that nature creates master races and slave races. Only the former have creative ability; the others are devoid of independence, cannot exist without foreign guidance, cannot evolve to a higher stage, but are doomed to serve the master races.

But the law of natural necessity with which these race theoreticians operate also affords additional pleasant inferences for certain bourgeois cliques of our time. Even within the master races there are differences of race, the blond race being the most magnificent of all. These blond (Nordic) gentlemen proclaim themselves to be the cleverest, noblest and mightiest of men, whom all others must serve. International politics must be based on this conception, from which also results the necessity for the existence of exploiters and exploited.

Viewed from this standpoint, the French Revolution assumes a very peculiar function. Mr. Bornhak, Professor of Public Law at the University of Berlin, begins with the fact that the area of present-day France, formerly inhabited by Celts, and later conquered by the Romans, finally succumbed during the migration of nations to Teutonic tribes, who there created a new government authority, controlled by them with the aid of the Catholic Church. This state appears to Bornhak as the exclusive achievement of the Teutonic barbarians: "The Celts are politically one of the most incapable races that have ever existed." The Teutons, on the other hand, are "a truly state-organising race of creative endowment". It is they who made France a power, until their Celtic subjects exterminated the master race in the great revolution, "with barbarous cruelty".

"The Romanised Celtic race becomes the entire population. But this result simultaneously, owing to the political incapacity of the Celtic race, sealed the fate of the French nation." [2]

The same conception of the French Revolution as a rebellion of inferior Celts against the noble blond race had previously been advocated by Driesmans, who maintained that this revolution had been "made by lawyers and journalists", professions of "unquestioned Celtic origin".[3] That is the way our race theoreticians understand the writing of history.

Their political economy is not any sounder. The anthropologist Ammon in 1893 published a work on natural selection among humans (*Die natürliche Auslese beim Menschen*), in which he finds, on the basis of material collected in Baden, that the class distinction between capitalists and proletarians is based on the existence of two races within the population, a blond, dolichocephalic, Teutonic race, and a black, brachycephalic, "Mongolian" race. The latter are declared deficient in independence and mental endowment, differing in these respects from the Teutons: "Like all Aryans, the Teutons are born to rule

[2] C. Bornhak: *Der Einfluss der Rasse auf die Staatsbildung,* "Archiv für Rassen- und Gesellschaftsbiologie", March, 1904, pp. 254 *et seq.*

[3] Quoted by Hertz: *Moderne Rassentheorien,* p. 10.

other peoples. Wherever they appear, they are the ruling and socially preferred classes, they are a people of fierce courage and indomitable energy, of devotion and fidelity, of pride and truthfulness, a shining race of demigods, the like of whom the world has seen but once before, in the Greeks, and will probably never see again."

Ammon investigates the story of the evolution of these demigods on the basis of material collected in the little province of Baden, where they live in the country as peasants together with the Mongolian roundheads, and emigrate to the cities like the latter. In the cities, owing to their demigod nature, they soon rise to splendid eminence, being transfigured into city employees, brewers, grain dealers, and other god-like forms, while the black-haired Asiatics from the Schwarzwald are relegated to the well deserved, contemptible servitude of wage-labour.

About the same time, even antedating Ammon, other theoreticians of race came forward with the statement that it was not the blond Teutons but the black-haired Asiatics who were more and more gaining control of capital in the cities, subjugating the Teutons and gradually displacing them even as intellectuals, physicians, lawyers, journalists. But the victors in this case were not lauded as demigods, but denounced as a dangerous riff-raff, who must be driven out or at least disfranchised, in the interest of the lordly Teutons. This race of swarthy undesirables is that of the *Jews*. The race argument is used more in support of anti-Semitism than in any other social movement of our times, having now completely displaced the religious argument in western Europe.

The anti-Semitism inherited from the Feudal Era had long seemed to be about to disappear, having dwindled to the same extent, and under the influence of the same capitalist evolution, as the power of religion, and being regarded as one of the prejudices of backward persons.

But about a generation ago it began to come up again, becoming modernised, and while it may not be a political factor in modern countries, it is nevertheless everywhere a social factor. We shall learn subsequently the causes of this condition, as well as why we shall not be able to dispose of this anti-Semitism so quickly, but also—of course —why anti-Semitism cannot count on a victory.

Let us first consider only the racial argument of anti-Semitism, an argument which is not used by anti-Semitism alone, but also by other domestic and international movements.

Characteristically enough, there is rising within Judaism, as a reaction against anti-Semitism, a similar tendency to accept and utilize the theory of race. It is a natural application of the principle: If this theory permits Christian-Teutonic patriots to declare themselves demigods, why should Zionist patriots not use it in order to stamp the people chosen by God as a chosen race of nature, a noble race that must be carefully guarded from any deterioration and contamination by foreign elements? A considerable literature has been produced within the past decade dealing

17

with questions of this order. Already in 1904, these arguments were well summarised and evaluated in Friedrich Hertz's book on modern theories of race,[4] of which a second revised and much enlarged edition was printed under another title in 1915.[5] Among the latest books on this subject, one of the best is that of Dr. Maurice Fishberg: *The Jews: A Study of Race and Environment*, London and New York, 1911, 578 pp.[6]

Fishberg uses not only material collected by other anthropologists, but also much new data obtained by him by measuring more than four thousand Jews from four continents, and digesting this material in a most conscientious and scholarly manner. It was to the many suggestions given me by this book that I owe the idea of writing the present little work.

In this connection, I might mention that I am again placed in the same embarrassing position that was mine when I wrote my book *Increase and Evolution in Nature and Society*, and to which I referred on pages vii and 17 of that work:[7] namely, I am obliged, although I am a layman in this field, to discuss questions connected with the

---

[4] Hertz: *Moderne Rassentheorien*, Vienna, 1904.

[5] *Rasse und Kultur*, Leipzig.

[6] Kautsky uses the German translation of L. Hepner: *Die Rassenmerkmale der Juden, Eine Einführung in ihre Anthropologie*, München, 1913, 800 pp. Our references are to the pages of the English edition, except where the German translation, which involved some changes, is specifically mentioned.—TRANSLATOR.

[7] *Vermehrung und Entwicklung in Natur und Gesellschaft*, Stuttgart, 1908.

natural science of biology. Here also there is a border region, one of the many points at which biology and sociology meet, and which, strictly speaking, would require the writer to be a master in both fields. But the present state of knowledge makes this impossible for any living man. No one who enters such a field—and they are much entered —can be required to have a mastery of more than one of the sciences in question, together with so much knowledge of the other as to know the general state of the science. His own science must always be such a man's point of departure; it is his task to show the agreement between the conclusions of his own science and those of the border science, which is by no means a simple matter—let us say— for a sociologist, who finds the specialists in natural science in such great disagreement in questions of race, as, for instance, on the fundamental problem of heredity. The sociologist may, therefore, consider himself justified in making his selection among the conflicting theories of the natural scientist, though he be a layman, and to favour such theory as may be compatible with the firm basis he has gained in sociology.

CHAPTER II

RACES OF ANIMALS

a. *Domestic Animals*

ONE of the most remarkable peculiarities of our theoreticians of race, who call themselves "anthropo-sociologists", is the fact that they leave us all the more in the
dark as to the true nature of the concept of race, the more
they have occasion to manipulate with this concept in the
explanation of social phenomena. A man's being, action,
performance, are due in their opinion simply to his race;
they have been inherited from his ancestors and are transmitted with the certainty of natural law to his descendants.
Race is the modern Fate, as inscrutable and immutable as
the latter.

It seems self-evident to the anthropo-sociological theoreticians of race that those groups designated as human
races should be understood in the same way as we understand races of animals. They seem to be not troubled for
a moment by any question as to whether the life conditions
of man do not alter the concept of race as applied to man.
They do not even take up the question of which type of
animal race is represented by the human races.

As a matter of fact, the races of animals are not all of
the same type, but may be divided into two different

groups: the *races of domestic animals,* and the *races of animals in the wild state.*

Zoologists and botanists distinguish these groups with great care. As a rule, they apply the word "race" only to the former, while the latter are termed "varieties" or "species". The theoreticians of race, the anthroposociologists, however, indiscriminately apply observations and laws valid for both the races of domestic animals as well as for the varieties of wild animals, to the human races. This alone must give rise to dreadful confusion, altogether aside from the fact that human beings are neither domestic animals nor animals in the wild condition, but a tribe living under quite peculiar conditions, conditions which do not resemble those of any other animals.

Before taking up the problem of race, we must therefore first attain clarity as to the distinction between the "race" of the domestic animal and the "variety" of the wild animal. We speak here only of animals, since only they are of importance to our problem, which concerns the human races, but the following remarks apply just as well to plants as to animals.

A phenomenon is best understood when its origin is known. In the case of the races of domestic animals, it is not difficult to ascertain this origin, for the process is being accomplished daily before our eyes. The breeding of new races is constantly going on. On the other hand, the formation of varieties in nature cannot be observed; it must be inferred as an hypothesis.

ARE THE JEWS A RACE?

If we regard the organisms in nature, we shall find that none of them serves a purpose lying outside of itself, but that each is an end in itself. Its individual organs must serve for the preservation of the whole, and must therefore be adequate for—or at least compatible with—self-preservation. An organism constituted otherwise cannot continue to exist, and certainly not to multiply.

But in the case of the animal organism, not only its own organs are important, but also those of other organisms with which it comes in contact, which oppose it, or on which it lives. Only man, however, has advanced to the point of altering in such manner the organs of the organisms from which or by which he lives, as to make them more subservient to his purposes. This is one of the means by which he has advanced beyond his primitive condition.

His first step in this process is to cause animals (also plants) which he would otherwise be obliged to seek out and capture with more or less difficulty, to live and multiply in his proximity. His first object in this is probably merely to diminish the difficulties of seeking, perhaps also of overcoming, the organisms on which he lives. But once the latter have been accustomed to live together with man as tame companions, man is also impelled to attempt to adapt the organs of the domestic animal, or of the cultivated plant, to his own purposes, for which nature did not intend them.

This is best attained by adequately altering their conditions of life, by increasing their supply of food, perhaps

22

by fertilizing or battening, decreasing their expenditure of strength in the life process, for instance, by sparing them the necessity of looking for fodder, of fleeing from enemies, of losing heat in the winter cold, etc. But, ultimately, man comes to the point of altering these organisms by making use of his observation that each individual has the tendency to transmit his qualities to his posterity. Much as all the individuals of the same species may resemble each other, they are never completely identical. Slight variations are always present, and these may easily be transmitted.

Most domestic animals finally become so amenable to man's guidance that he is enabled to mate them, or prevent them from reproducing, as he likes. Once he has advanced to this point, he will, of course, prefer to permit those specimens to reproduce that are most suitable for his purposes, that furnish most milk, meat, or fat, or yield the finest wool, or lay most eggs, have most traction power or swiftness, etc. If those of their posterity continue to reproduce, who present these qualities in the most emphatic form, these qualities will gradually be reinforced to such an extent, and the bodies of the animals will alter so greatly, as to be perceptibly different from those of their ancestors, thus producing a new species from the old species, with permanent, repeatedly transmittable characteristics, provided the breeding-animals are always mated only with their like.

This selection is at first predominantly an unconscious

one. The best specimens are reproduced because they are most prized. Without any intention of securing a new race, this final outcome of the process has not been apparent from the outset. But the art of breeding is perfected more and more, becomes more and more conscious, and finally actually sets out to create specific races with specific race traits. At times, new variations may sporadically appear in isolated specimens. If these are of advantage to man, he will attempt to reproduce them. Thus, in 1791, a ram with short, crooked legs and a long back, which was thus prevented from jumping over hedges, gave rise to a new race in America, that of the Ancona sheep. Likewise in France in 1828, a hornless ram with uncommonly soft, long wool, led to the creation of a new race, the Mauchamp sheep. As a rule, however, the creation of a new race is not such a simple matter, but proceeds by means of a slow, gradual reinforcement of traits, often discernible in the first generation only to the trained eye of experienced breeders, and not attaining practical significance until they have been reinforced to a sufficient extent in the course of generations.

The uninterrupted selection of breeding-animals, continued for generations according to the same plan, creates a new race which is maintained by the fact that only such specimens are reproduced as present this race trait in the most emphatic form, that a mating with individuals of other races is strictly avoided, and all specimens of the specific race which present a variation that deviates from the desired race trait are of course excluded from further breeding.

The necessary condition for the formation of such new races is, of course, that the animals reproduce in the tame state and that their mating be under man's control. The elephant, as a rule, reproduces only in the wild state and has created no new races.

On the other hand, the domestic cat leaves nothing to be desired in the way of prolificness, yet the cat has preserved much of its original freedom in spite of man. Its love-life is carried on not in the stable but on the roofs, and therefore, according to Darwin, it does not furnish any different races within the same country.[1]

However, the formation of new races under otherwise identical circumstances will be the easier, the greater the certainty to mate specific individuals, and the more swiftly the generations succeed each other. This is the reason for the great increase of races of rabbits and pigeons; here the breeding of such races has become a sport.

b. *Wild Animals*

Let us now examine the case of the formation of varietie of animals in the wild condition, which should—it woul appear—have been examined before we took up the race of domestic animals, for the wild varieties, of course, aros

[1] Charles Darwin, *The Variation of Animals and Plants und Domestication*, London, 1876, vol. i, pp. 45, 46; vol. ii, pp. 220, 222.

earlier and constitute the fundamental trunk from which the races of domestic animals have branched off. But in a study of the *history* of the *theory* of the evolution of races, the origin of the organisms controlled by man is the proper point of departure, for it was the observations made in artificial selection that led Darwin to construct his hypothesis of natural selection.

Darwin assumed that the formation of varieties and species proceeds in the natural condition, as in the case of domestic animals and cultivated plants, by a selection of the best, most adapted, specimens for reproduction, and excluding from reproduction those less fitted, with the sole difference that the selection, in the natural condition, is not conducted by man, in accordance with his purposes, but by the struggle for existence, which is a consequence of overpopulation, of the circumstance that more individuals of each species are produced than can continue to exist. A constant merciless struggle is going on among them, in which the weakest, least fit, succumb, while the strongest, most fit, maintain themselves and reproduce. Serious objections were raised to this view at the very outset. If the struggle for existence is a continuous, progressive selection of the best specimens, the transformation of species must be going on continuously, and at a rather rapid rate. In the case of certain domestic animals and garden plants a specific new race may be produced in the course of a few years.

In nature, on the other hand, observation shows us that

species remain apparently unchanged for long periods. They may change in geological periods, but remain unchanged for many thousands of years within a geological period. In historical times, the great mass of wild animal species has remained entirely the same. As depicted on the ancient Egyptian and Assyrian monuments, they look exactly like their prototypes of today. We are told this difficulty may be eliminated by assuming that evolution proceeds with tremendous slowness, by a gradual accumulation of imperceptible alterations. But the slower this evolution, the more imperceptible the alterations contributed to progress by each generation, the more insurmountable becomes another difficulty in the theory of selection: it becomes more and more impossible to assume that each alteration bestows upon the individual producing it a preponderance over other individuals not supplied with it. In artificial selection, the selection is made by men who already have in mind the new type that is to be bred, grasping its practical advantages and appreciating— through eyes that have been sharpened by this prophecy— the significance of hardly perceptible alterations, which are important not in themselves, but merely as points of departure in a long chain of development, the new type being realised only at its termination. The theory of evolution attempts to dispense altogether with providence in the formation of natural species. Without the aid of far-sighted selection, however, imperceptible alterations cannot become the cause for the survival and reproduction of the individuals supplied with them. Reference to artificial selection is here of no value at all.

In addition, we have a third difficulty: Darwin called his theory of natural selection an explanation of the origin of *species*. If correct, this theory would merely afford an explanation of the evolution of more highly organised *individuals* from those less highly organised. Its whole emphasis is laid on the solution of the problem of *evolution*. But, in order to explain the origin of species, we must also explain the *similarity* between individuals, which leads to generalising them as a specific species. Whence this similarity?

In the case of artificial selection, the cause of the similarity between individuals is in their common descent from the same ancestors. The ancestral tree is here of great importance. But it is impossible, in this case, to maintain a "pure race" without constant intervention on the part of the breeder, who must carefully guard his race animals against mating with others, and who must eliminate from their posterity all those individuals that present alterations deviating from the pure racial type.

In nature this breeder is lacking. Unless the alterations are of such variety as to doom the individual to early destruction, they will not prevent it from mating with other differently constituted individuals, and thus from reproducing. A constant mingling of individuals with the most varied changes will take place.

A breeder producing a new race, furthermore, is concerned only with a specific one-sided peculiarity, which he aims to perpetuate. His selection is made solely with this object in view. But in nature, it is not merely a single quality which affords advantage to the individuals possessing it; the most varied qualities may be of value. Let us assume the theory of selection to be correct to the extent that evolution takes place by reason of the fact that individuals with advantageous alterations maintain and reproduce themselves more easily than others. Even here, the most varied alterations are possible, as we may see from the case of the hare. Some hares will be benefited by longer legs, others by greater endurance, a third variety by better protective mimicry (perhaps they are white in winter and brown in summer), a fourth group by reason of enhanced productiveness, others again through increased power of resistance to climatic influences (perhaps they have a thick pelt in winter, a light one in summer); finer differences in the sense organs, sharper eyes, better hearing, finer sense of smell, as well as differences in intelligence, in swiftness and correctness of the judgments based on sensual impressions, will be of advantage. One individual may present one set of advantages, another may have other advantages.

If only such individuals should continue to mate as have coincident traits, they might emphasise these traits and thus create a new race. But since there are many such traits, a single species within the same region would not give rise to a single new species but to many such. Thus, as contrasted with wild rabbits, tame rabbits may be divided into many races.

But a mating limited to individuals of the same peculiarities is impossible in the wild state. The character of the mates there depends entirely on accident, on the mating of certain individuals at the moment of the mating season. There is not always sexual selection; mating is often promiscuous. Where there is such selection, it is limited to one sex. The victorious stag will have relations with all the does of his herd, regardless of their properties. And the selection—if present at all—is carried out among a small number only.

In the wild state, therefore, the most varied deviations will be transmitted within a certain species. These deviations continue to mingle again. It is impossible to see how natural selection can here produce new important species with coincident traits. If a constant progressive evolution takes place owing to the survival of the fittest, with new properties and by means of their transmission, this evolution must lead to a disintegration of existing species into a confused mass of varying individuals, all similarity among which will progressively disappear. The theory of the *origin* of species becomes a theory of their dissolution, and it remains impossible to grasp how species based on the similarity of numerous individuals should ever arise. But, as a matter of fact, we find in nature many more individuals having coincident traits than we do among domestic animals. We have already pointed out how great is the number of races of tame rabbits, as compared with the uniformity found among wild rabbits and field hares.

And the number of species of wild animals is not increasing, while almost each new year supplies us with a new race in the case of many domestic animals:

"But geology shows us, that from an early part of the tertiary period the number of species of shells, and that from the middle part of this same period the number of mammals, has not greatly or at all increased." [2]

In the introduction to his fine book on the distribution of the animal world, Kobelt says: "I have not been able to convince myself that a sole, uniform transformation of the animal kingdom is taking place over long periods, as a strict interpretation of Darwinism would require. . . . Beginning with the middle pliocene period (the geological period immediately preceding the origin of man —K.), we cannot prove with any degree of certainty the new origin of any species." [3]

Whence then the great similarity between so many individuals in the wild state?

We cannot explain this similarity by considering only the individual and the evolution of the individual. We are here dealing with a *mass phenomenon*, which may be explained only by means of a factor lying outside of the individuals, above them, influencing them all in the same manner. It is not hard to discover this factor if we con-

[2] Charles Darwin, *The Origin of Species*, Harvard Classics Edition, chap. iv, p. 140.

[3] *Die Verbreitung der Tierwelt*, Leipzig, 1902.

sider the varieties of animals in the natural state. Among races of domestic animals, the individual ancestors, the ancestral tree, is of importance. But the varieties of wild animals are "geographical races". This is true even for the domestic cat, which resists artificial breeding; it is all the more true of animals in the unrestrained, natural state.

Thus, among lions, we may distinguish the varieties of the Barbary lion, the Senegal lion, the Cape lion, the Persian lion, the Guzerat lion. Among elephants, we distinguish between the Indian and the African. Rhinoceroses are divided into several varieties: the Indian rhinoceros, "whose area of distribution seems limited to the Indian peninsula"; the Varana rhinoceros, "as far as our knowledge goes, is found only in Java". "The half-armored rhinoceros is found only in Sumatra (*Cerator hinus sumatrensis*)." "The area of distribution of the double-horned rhinoceros (*Atelodus bicornis* and *Atelodus simus*) now extends over all of Central Africa." "The hornless rhinoceros is said now to be limited to the southern half of Africa." [4]

Similarly in the case of the hare: "All of central Europe and a small portion of western Asia is the home of the Continental hare. In the south, it is the *Mediterranean hare*, a deviating species of small size and reddish color; in the high mountains, it is the *Alpine hare*, in the far north, the *snow hare*. . . . The African hares differ from ours by their smaller size and also by their uncommonly long ears." [5]

---

[4] Brehm: *Tierleben*.   [5] *Ibid.*

RACES OF ANIMALS

In other words, it is the geographical differences which produce the differences between varieties in the natural state: differences in climate, configuration of the soil, the nature of the nutrition and the mode of obtaining it, the species of enemies, etc. On the other hand, it is the *uniformity of the conditions of life* within a certain region which produces the similarity between the individuals of the species concerned. This similarity is more powerful than the differences, the variations of the individuals. The latter tend to be dissimilar, to diverge. The conditions of life in nature, in a certain region, are the same, however, for all, operate in the same way, and oppose the tendency to diverge.

If we thus consider the conditions of life, the milieu, as the decisive factor in the moulding of varieties and species in the natural state, we are eliminating the difficulties that would arise if we should proceed—in our explanation of natural varieties—from the experiences obtained in the breeding of the races of domestic animals.

We are now enabled to understand not only the similarity of the individuals of the same species within a certain region, but also the constancy, the tendency to immutability, of species in historical times, as well as their alterations in geological periods. As long as the milieu remains the same, the species will not change. But the milieu does not permanently remain the same. The earth changes, alters its position in the firmament. Passing through space, together with the entire solar system, it may at times encounter colder regions, at other times warmer ones, in what we call the universe. Nor is its position always the same with regard to the sun; its axis oscillates, and many portions of the earth's surface may thus obtain a more polar climate than formerly, while others obtain a more equatorial climate.

Far more certain than these changes are those arising from the gradually growing coldness of the earth, its gradual shrinking. Continents and oceans are formed, some of the latter deep, others shallow; flat lands and mountains, marine currents and trade winds, nothing permanent, everything changing, but changing only in endless periods. For thousands of years the same condition will prevail in a certain region; then it will gradually change; moisture yields to drought, warmth to cold, low plains are lifted up, twisted into mountain chains, or subside and furnish sea bottoms. When such changes ensue, the organisms of the region cannot remain the same. Some are destroyed, some are driven out, forced to migrate, some adapt themselves to the new conditions, which they may do in many ways, for which Lamarck and Darwin, as well as their disciples, have gathered very interesting illustrations. But once the organisms of the region are adapted to the new condition of affairs, we no longer find any cause for further changes of their condition, and they will remain in their new forms until new changes in their life conditions are introduced.

This is not a new view. Darwin himself, in the historical sketch introducing his book on the origin of species, points

out that Isidore Geoffroy Saint-Hilaire had stated it to
be his opinion (in 1850) of the traits of species, "that
they are permanent for each species so long as it reproduces itself within the same conditions, but that they
change when the external conditions of life change".

Darwin fully recognised the effect of the altered conditions of life as well as of the use or non-use of organs. But
he underestimated their importance, since he was completely dominated by the observations made in artificial
selection, and by the assumption of a constant struggle for
existence under the pressure of overpopulation. This latter view he owed to Malthus; it is still considered a cast-
iron law of natural science.

But if we examine the struggle for existence, we shall
find that overpopulation—in other words, the struggle between individuals of the same species for fodder—plays
but a small rôle, is only an exceptional phenomenon.

A few concrete examples will help us. Hares, as is well
known, are very fruitful. The female hare gives birth to a
number of young as early as the month of March; very few
of these survive; how many, depends chiefly on the weather.
Snow, freezing weather, will destroy almost all of them.
Sunshine, warm breezes, will enable many to live. It is
clear that in these cases the selection among the young
hares is but little concerned with the number struggling
for existence. The struggle here amounts to a struggle
against the external conditions of life, not against numerous competitors of the same species.

Or, let us consider antelopes in an African steppe. Sometimes there is drought for many weeks; springs run dry, pools of water evaporate, many antelopes die of thirst. Only those remain alive which can bear thirst longest, or whose organs are so delicate as to enable them to sense the presence of water at great distances, better than the other antelopes. The struggle for existence here certainly produces an extensive selection, but it is a struggle against the external conditions of life, and has nothing to do with the number of antelopes. The quantity of water did not become insufficient because it was drunk by too many antelopes.

Another enemy of the antelopes is the lion. But the lion's strength and cruelty do not depend upon the number of antelopes. There may even ensue a struggle between two lions for a single antelope, if there are not many antelopes, the stronger lion being victorious. But even this is of rare occurrence.

Far from being the general and constant cause of the struggle for existence, the great fruitfulness of certain organisms is rather a weapon enabling them to maintain themselves in this struggle, in which they would otherwise succumb. The struggle for existence, as a rule, is not a struggle between members of the same species when it has become too numerous, but a struggle of the individual or a group of individuals of the same species against the external conditions of life, which include not only the inorganic surroundings, but also the organic surroundings.

Changes in these conditions of life also involve changes in the mode of the struggle for existence, in the method of using the organs; old organs or forms of organs become dispensable, new organs, or new forms of old organs, become necessary. If the species succeeds in evolving in the struggle with the new conditions, and thus becoming a new species, it will maintain itself; otherwise it will be destroyed. We may judge from remains found in the bowels of the earth how many such species have been destroyed in the earth's history.

The theory of overpopulation proves nothing, therefore, against the assumption that the final cause for the formation of new species is in the changes of the conditions of life. Another view must still be mentioned: the view that acquired characteristics cannot be inherited.

Modern physiologists distinguish between the body cells and the reproductive cells, the "body plasm" and the "germ plasm". The germ plasm, according to their view, is immutable, being transmitted again and again. But, according to Weismann, it is immutable even to the extent that it is not influenced by the qualities acquired by the body of the individual during his life. The individual cannot, therefore, transmit these acquisitions. Thus the formation of new, transmittable traits of species by the influence of new conditions of life on the body, is precluded. But this view was emphatically opposed, from its first appearance, particularly by Darwinists. Darwin, himself, assumed the heredity of acquired characteristics, as did also Herbert Spencer. Recent experiments show, on the one hand, that external influences do produce changes which are transmitted, and, on the other hand, that the germ plasm is by no means absolutely independent of the body plasm. This question is excellently treated by Tschulok in his little book on evolution; the following experiment is particularly interesting:

"Two races of hens were treated, one pure black, the other pure white. The races were pure, *i.e.*, it was known definitely for each individual that its parents, grandparents and great-grandparents had all presented the same characteristics as the individual itself; in other words, that no mixture had taken place. When such a white hen was crossed with a white cock, their posterity were white exclusively. Similarly, mating a black hen with a black cock produced only black posterity.

"Now the following experiment was made:

"The ovary of a white hen was removed and implanted in the body of a black hen; the black hen's ovary was also implanted in the white hen. The operation was performed so neatly that the animals remained alive and were capable, after the wounds had healed, of producing posterity by the normal methods. The white hen with the black ovary was now fructified by a black cock. We should here expect the posterity to be black, for the ova in the ovary of the white hen came from a black hen, and the male semen was likewise obtained from a black cock. However, the chickens were colored black and white. Similarly, the black hen, with an ovary taken from a white hen, was fructified by a white cock. The posterity included not only pure white chickens, but also chickens with black spots." [6]

This result is the more astonishing in that it was attained by powerful mechanical interference, not by a gradual, organic alteration. The ovary in the body of the black hen had already attained full development when it was implanted in the white hen's body, and yet the influence of the new body cells on the transferred germ cells was so strong as to enable the new body fully to impress its type upon the ovary. It might be assumed that the influence of changed somatic traits on the germ plasm must be still stronger in cases where the body suffers changes by reason of the influence of altered conditions, before its germ cells attain full maturity, with the result that the process of maturing goes on completely under the influence of the new properties.

We, therefore, see no reason that would oblige us to assume that acquired characteristics cannot be transmitted. The manner in which heredity works is, however, still completely hidden. Nor may we assume that all acquired characteristics are inherited. Lesions and mutilations, for instance, are hardly transmitted. Weismann cut off the tails of many generations of mice, without ever obtaining a tailless mouse. Many an apparent case of heredity may also be explained by the fact that the posterity live under the same conditions as their ancestors,

[6] Tschulok, *Entwicklungstheorie,* Stuttgart, J. H. W. Dietz, 1912.

and therefore acquire and present the same characteristics, without necessarily inheriting them.

There are many degrees among the inherited characteristics. Some are more persistent than others. There are inherited characteristics which the individual may easily lose if it enters a milieu deviating from that producing these qualities. Other traits, on the other hand, are stubbornly retained for many generations, even with the greatest variations in the conditions of life. Relatively, as compared with those traits that change easily, inherited traits of the latter kind may be considered immutable. But if they were acquired owing to the influence of special conditions of life, it would be impossible to understand why they should not be capable of changing under the influence of altered conditions of life.

Many scientists distinguish between race traits proper, in man, which are said to be absolutely unchanging, such as the color of the eyes, the hair, the skin, the shape of the skull; and secondary or fluctuating properties, such as bodily stature, bone structure, muscular system, fatty tissue, etc.

No doubt there is a difference between race traits of these two kinds. But perhaps this difference should be ascribed solely to the fact that the conditions bringing about the fluctuating properties are more susceptible and more swiftly susceptible to change than those causing the apparently immutable race traits. The former may change so quickly as to enable us to observe their influence without difficulty. The other conditions we do not even know, perhaps for the reason that they do not change perceptibly within the period of our observations. But we cannot say of any race trait that it is absolutely unchanging; such a trait would be the sole unchanging phenomenon in this changing world.

On this point, Fishberg says:

"Recent investigations have led to a modification or even complete abandonment of the theory of the constancy and persistence of race traits. For a long time, some anthropologists have maintained that the external environment, particularly the nutrition, the social and geographical surroundings, have a powerful influence on the modification of some traits, such as musculature, stature, etc. Many even go so far as to say that these agencies may alter pigmentation and head-form. Ridgeway, going further, assumes that the duration of human types in a certain region, and over long periods, is an expression not of the influence of heredity, but of environment, and that, on the other hand, modifications of the human form found in the Mediterranean region, and in central and northwest Africa, may be traced back to differences of climate, soil and national products.

"This theory of the decisive influence of environment on the alteration or modification of basic somatic traits may easily be applied to some of the race traits. . . . In some regions it has been found that the soil has a powerful influence on the stature of the inhabitants; for instance, the great height of persons inhabiting the State of Kentucky is very probably to be explained by the presence of hard water in this region. Similarly (according to Röse), the stature of the population in Gotha, Germany, has been undergoing changes since the introduction of hard water. Observations have also been made on the influence of environment on the head-form—a trait that has hitherto been considered immutable under all circumstances. . . .

"Professor Franz Boas, of New York, recently arrived at the conclusion, based on his investigations, that the absolute persistence of human types is an untenable theory. His investigations of the physical characteristics of immigrants have revealed an extremely interesting condition; he finds that the children of immigrants are of higher stature and better bodily development than their parents born in Europe. He has also discovered a very remarkable alteration in the head-form of children born in America after their parents had landed. Even a child born abroad, and not more than one year old on its arrival in America, will retain the foreign head-form. But a child born in America, though only a few months after the parents have landed, has the American head-form." [7]

Other investigators before Boas had found that the whites in the United States acquire more and more Indian traits in the course of a few generations, thus becoming "Indianized".

But it would be premature to infer from these facts that

[7] Fishberg, German edition, pp. 5 *et seq.*

tne American milieu will ultimately make Indians of the whites.

Even among animals, the milieu is only one of the circumstances determining somatic forms and physical strength. Other things being equal, these conditions will produce both; but these conditions also include the organism on which the milieu is working. The same milieu will not necessarily influence different organisms in the same way, but may have different effects on each. If various races are transplanted from the milieus producing them, into a new environment, they will all be changed by this environment, but not necessarily all in the same way.

The American conditions may have a different effect on a white man than on a Mongolian or on a Negro.

Other factors enter also, however, which make the race problem in the case of man much more complicated even than among animals.

CHAPTER III

THE RACES OF MAN

WE have found that the races of animals in the natural condition, and the races of domestic animals, are two very different things. It would, therefore, be erroneous to apply to one of these groups observations made in the case of the other.

The pure race of domestic animals may always be traced back to a specific *parent couple*. A specific race (variety) of wild animals may be traced to a certain *region*. The naïve view of primitive peoples derived each species of wild animals from a specific parent couple—as they also derived each nation from such a couple. When the Deluge was impending, Noah, in order to preserve the animal creation, took of each species "a male and his female" into the Ark, later liberating them again. We are not told how the carnivorous animals kept alive when only two specimens of each variety of herbivorous animals were available.

Primitive though this view may be, it still prevails to a great extent even in present-day thinking. In the case of related varieties and species, we still speak of a "common blood", a common descent.

Darwin says: "All the individuals of the same species, and all the species of the same genus, or even higher group, *must have descended from common parents;* and therefore, in however distant and isolated parts of the world they are now found, they must, in the course of successive generations, have passed from some one part to the others." [1]

This common descent from a single parent couple, which may be observed in races produced artificially, is extremely improbable in the case of natural species.

We know nothing of the origin of life, but we must assume that, like all other phenomena, this origin is subject to the law that like causes under like circumstances will always produce like effects. As soon as the conditions and causes of organic life were present on earth, it is not probable that an isolated speck of albumen took shape, with living functions, multiplying its number by growth and fission, thus becoming the parent of all existing organisms, but we must assume that primitive organisms, however we may conceive their shape—were formed in all places in which the conditions for their existence were given—and that they immediately expanded and peopled their entire "nutrition area". They began to multiply as soon as suitable areas were available, and they began to assume varying forms as these areas, and with them the conditions of life, became more manifold. Each new higher species therefore must have been present in numerous specimens from its very beginning.

And we must make this assumption even in the case of the highest forms. We have no evidence that humanity

[1] Charles Darwin, *The Origin of Speeies,* New York, 1860, p. 400.

ıs descended from a single couple of ape-men. It is more probable that the evolution proceeded on the basis of an entire species of ape-like animals, which had become subject to conditions bringing about their development into humans. Common racial traits among animals in the natural condition do not therefore by any means point to a common origin—not to the remotest degree—in a single parent couple, and therefore not to blood relationship. But it may be assumed that a great number of them are more or less closely related. The number of blood relations within a variety will probably be the greater, the longer this variety has been in existence and the smaller the territory now inhabited by it.

The varieties of an animal species in the natural state within a certain region are extremely limited; therefore, there is only one such variety in a specific region, and this variety does not change as long as the conditions of the region remain the same. The races of a species of domestic animals within a certain region may, on the other hand, be quite numerous. They are being constantly transformed, become constantly more numerous, and become more and more different from the primitive race from which they take their origin.

This condition is brought about by the fact that man is able to provide an artificial environment for the animal races shaped by him, thus abolishing in great measure the effects of the natural environment. In the case of animals in the natural state, the organism is adapted to its life

46

conditions: in the case of domestic conditions, the life conditions are adapted to the organism which man is breeding in accordance with his needs. High-breed domestic animals could probably no longer exist without the aid of man.

This new kind of adaptation—not of the organism to its environment, but of the environment to the organism—conducted by man for his domestic animals, he, of course, applies in the highest degree when dealing with himself. It is this process which causes man to cease to be a wild animal, but it does not make him a domestic animal.

In the accommodation of its life conditions to the organism, the domestic animal is purely passive; this adaptation is undertaken *by man for the animal.* Man is the active element in the process. But the animal ceases to be an end in itself. Its organism becomes subservient to the purposes of man. But, like the animal in the wild state, man knows no higher end than himself; he alters his milieu *to suit himself.*

To be sure, the purpose served by man may not be exclusively his own personality. Even among animals in the natural state there are social animals, among whom the individual cannot exist for itself alone, or at least it cannot exist fully for itself alone; each is obliged to cooperate with others; its welfare depends on the welfare of the social group to which it belongs. Society is higher than the individual; its purposes are higher than those of the individual.

ARE THE JEWS A RACE?

Even in the animal world, the dependence of the individual on the group to which it belongs is carried to a high stage. It is probably not an accident that precisely those animal species were best fitted to become domestic animals which were able to subordinate their individuality to an outer compulsion. In the case of man, the social cohesion, owing to language and economy, is much closer than in most animals—perhaps excepting bees and ants. The individual's dependence on society increases. But great as may be the occasional contradiction between the interests of the totality and those of the individual, in the case of man, the social interests are always human interests, and are therefore always directly or indirectly the interests of the individual himself. We are here dealing with a primitive, simple society, and are therefore disregarding class differences.

Removal from the natural state usually has not the same effect on man as on the other animals. This removal is man's own work, the product of his knowledge of the conditions of life, of his mental superiority over the rest of organic nature. It is the outcome of his ability to strengthen and variegate his organs of sensual perception and motion by means of artificial organs, and thereby to surmount the obstacles in surrounding nature to a greater extent than he could in the natural condition, *i.e.*, aided by his bodily organs alone. Each new advance in this field, each victory over a natural barrier, makes man face a new difficulty, new problems, but also provides him with new, hitherto unknown means and knowledge for their solution. The natural environment to which the organisms of wild animals are adapted do not change in historical times, *i.e.*, as measured in human records. The artificial environment adapted by man to his own organism, has been changing considerably in historical times. Doubtless nature also is in constant flux, but the rate of change is imperceptible, as measured by the advances in the evolution of technology and social forms among men. The natural environment of wild animals may therefore be considered unchanging as compared with the constantly changing artificial environment of man.

This environment is adapted to the needs of the human organism. But it also has its effect on this organism. It makes no new demands on most of the bodily organs, perhaps even reduces the number of its former demands; for example, in the case of the teeth, which may deteriorate as a result. But it makes more and more demands on those organs which have created this environment, the organs of cognition and judgment, or, in other words, of mental activity in general.

In the natural state, the same situations repeat themselves again and again with very slight differences for each animal species, so long as no alterations ensue in the environment. The experiences, judgments and actions arising from these situations therefore tend to uniformity, to become fixed habits. And, like other acquired characteristics, habits practised for generations and turning out to be expedient for the organism, finally become hereditary; they become impulses, instincts, which are followed without thought.

In the case of man, the instinctive life is more and more forced into the background, as the natural environment is replaced by an artificial environment and as the changes in the latter proceed more and more rapidly, as they introduce more and more new problems, which cannot be solved without careful investigation. The organs of mental activity are therefore made to deal with more and more varied new tasks, are put to more and more exertion and thus develop more and more. The demands made upon the mental organs are of increasing complexity and variety; likewise, the manner in which these organs are called upon to act. Simultaneously, the relations of men to each other, both between individuals and tribes, become quite varied, with the result that the most manifold possibilities arise for mental development. The organs of the human spirit become the most valuable, but also the most adaptable of all organs, those subject to the swiftest and most powerful transformations.

We find an opposite evolutionary trend among domestic animals, the development of whose organs depends on man. But from most of these animals man asks only more meat, milk, wool, eggs, traction power; he rarely asks increased intelligence, never independent judgment. Aside from dogs, the progress of breeding, in the case of domestic animals, is accompanied by a decrease of intelligence, and even in the case of the dog, it is doubtful whether the "noblest" races are also the most intelligent.

As man's intelligence and technology improve, he becomes more able to offer resistance to the influences of the life conditions surrounding him. He may, therefore, when geographical conditions change, maintain his hereditary somatic traits, his racial peculiarities, better than in the natural condition. This reduces the effect of accommodation in man, and emphasises that of heredity. But this applies only to the somatic traits in the narrower sense, not to the organs of mental life, which, when enhanced in sensitiveness and variability, at once react to any alteration in the life conditions.

But in the case of man, a change, not only in the artificial conditions of life, but also in those that are natural, may easily ensue, while such changes are rare in the natural state. In nature, we have usually only slow changes, alterations over geological periods, such as in ice ages, in the rising and subsiding of continents, which cause important and permanent migrations of animal species. Such processes take place so slowly that the organisms concerned are eliminated almost imperceptibly, step by step, thus facilitating their adaptation to the new conditions of neighbouring regions. Man, however, acquires means of locomotion enabling him to cover great distances with increasing speed, and his technology in the winning of foodstuffs, the manufacturing of clothing, the construction of houses, the uses of fuel, illumination, etc., enable him to enter regions in which he could not possibly maintain himself in his natural state.

But with the possibility of undertaking swift and extended journeys, man's desire for such journeys is awakened. In the natural state, the fruitfulness of each species of organisms is adapted to its life conditions, with a resulting state of equilibrium between the various species. My book on increase and evolution takes up this question more in detail. I am here obliged merely to suggest this thought, like so many others.

Man's technology disturbs this condition of equilibrium. His fruitfulness is now subject to changing conditions, likewise his mortality. This may sometimes lead to the dying out of certain tribes, while at other times it may cause so extensive an increase as to deprive posterity of the necessary space in the home country. Later, the attraction of certain regions for strangers also is an element, even when such strangers are not driven from their homes by overpopulation. This attraction itself depends on the evolution of technology and economy and may be of varying nature. River constructions or improvements in navigation may render the shores of rivers or the coasts of oceans, formerly desolate and inaccessible, so attractive as to make them a goal for poorer tribes. In our own days, the gold resources of Alaska have caused a migration into that region.

The most varied causes and opportunities for migrations arise. The same race may now be found living in the most varied regions and climates. These migrations may proceed so swiftly, and be so temporary, as to preclude any possibility of the race's adaptation to the new conditions, its acquisition of new hereditary traits. But even when a migration leads to permanent settlement in a new region, the artificial environment created by man in that region will be so powerful as to enable it to resist the influence of the natural environment over periods that may be of relatively considerable duration.

We know nothing of man in the natural state. Even the most primitive men we know have a certain technology. We do not know whether man in the natural state inhabited only a specific region of uniform character, or several regions with varying character, whether he then constituted a single geographical race or several such. At any rate, his race character must have been entirely dependent on nature.

Technical and economic progress then creates two different tendencies. Increased impulses and opportunities for migrations induce many races gradually to spread over the most varied regions; the varying natural conditions of the new environments have an influence in the direction of substituting changed race traits for old race traits, of substituting for the old race, or placing by its side—if not all of the race has emigrated—a group of new races. The alteration in race traits takes place either directly, through the influence of natural factors: heat, cold, drought, moisture, light, darkness, etc.; or, indirectly, through the struggle against these factors, through the use of certain organs, disuse of others. Depending on the development of technology and of the social conditions, this struggle may assume different forms, and in the same region may therefore produce various race types among varying modes of production. If a steppe becomes inhabited by fugitive nomads, it will produce different traits in these nomads from those produced in a later population with a sufficiently developed technology to enable it to transform the steppe into fruitful farm land by means of irrigation, and therefore cultivating this land as a permanent peasantry.

Therefore, the advances in technology and the migrations increase the number of race differences and create new geographical races. On the other hand, however, technology, beyond a certain level, may retard the formation of such races. The higher the evolution of human technology, the more independent becomes the race of the nature of the environment. The race may maintain its character in the most varied regions, even such as have no similarity with the region in which the race originated. Thus, we find Europeans, Chinese, Negroes, in the most varied parts of the world, living under the most different climates.

But no matter how highly developed its technology, no race can permanently and completely escape from the influence of the environment. It may most easily escape from the organic environment, the flora and fauna, which may be changed rather easily by human intervention. On the other hand, the influence of telluric factors—altitude above sea level, configuration of the soil, quantity of sunlight, heat, cold—can never be entirely eliminated.

But even here our remarks refer only to somatic race traits proper. Even the most temporary change in the location of a race, producing no alteration in the physical appearance, may, by opening up new regions, with new conditions, produce new impressions, new problems, may not be without effect on the mental life, and therefore also on its organs, whose quality, like that of any organ, depends on the degree and nature of their use. The more diligently the race applies itself to resist the influence of the new milieu, the more its somatic race traits are thus retained, the more will its organs of mental life be exerted in a new manner and consequently be subject to change under the influence of the new environment.

The possibility that a race may pass beyond the geographical boundaries set up by nature, that therefore the human races may cease to be geographical races, like the varieties of animals in the natural state, often leads—and has led more and more of late—to the presence of a number of races in the same region, living together more or less amicably. There results a new possibility which is very exceptional in the natural state, namely, that of *race mixture*, which may at times lead to the creation of new races, but very often merely disintegrates the old races, for which it substitutes a conglomeration of the most varied ingredients. This process of race mixture has been going on for tens of thousands, perhaps hundreds of thousands, of years:

"The present presents millions of cases of this, as did also the past, and there is no such thing as an unmixed race on this small planet with its easy communications. . . . On this earth, all the races gradually merge into each other, and each race is composed of various subdivisions." [2]

The further a race is removed from its original habitations and its original conditions, the greater its migrations, the richer its history, the more developed its commerce; in other words, the higher its status, the more will be the opportunities it has had for race mixture, the less will it retain of its original "race"; the more has it ceased to be a "pure" race, and the more varied will be the race elements of other provenience which it has absorbed. Unless the rather permanent influence of uniform natural conditions in a certain region has opposed this manifold character and tended to create a new homogeneous geographical race, cross-breedings and atavism in such a population will produce the greatest variety of somatic, and particularly, of mental, traits, the latter being far more variable than the former. The higher the technical and social stages of evolution, therefore, the smaller will be the influence of the natural conditions.

But social progress produces not only a tendency to dissolve the old traditional forms, but also gives rise to

[2] Ratzel: *Anthropogeographie,* vol. ii, p. 587.

factors tending to create new types within a population.
This is brought about by the *division of labour*, which is
but rarely found in the animal kingdom—again excepting
bees and ants—but which attains considerable proportions
in human society and becomes one of the most important
bases of its progress.

The division into callings sometimes becomes a division
into classes, ruling and ruled classes, exploiting and exploited. The division of labour finally leads to a division
of society into workers and non-workers. Such divisions
result in the formation of groups within a people, each of
which makes use of its natural organs differently, or makes
use of different organs, and in their living each under different conditions, in a different environment. Under these
circumstances, each of these groups acquires its special
properties, sometimes somatic traits, but chiefly mental
traits, for the economic and social divisions create more
differences in mental aptitudes than of occupation in those
that are physical in the narrower sense.

We have already observed that the same race, by scat-
tering over various regions, with different modes of production, may suffer changes. We now find that the same
race, within the same region, may present such divisions,
owing to economic influences. On the other hand, similarity of occupation may impress the same trait upon members
of different races and tend to eliminate such differences as
may have been present.

Ratzel, for instance, observes: "In many cases, when we

speak of 'race', it would be better to speak of 'class'. Throughout all peoples, somatic differences accompany the division into castes, which division is the more emphatic, the further removed the races are from culture and freedom. . . . The distribution of skin pigment most frequently accompanies differences of castes, for obvious reasons. . . . We cannot trace the precise scale of colour dividing the upper and lower classes upon one and the same island. Cook and Forster state that the former are lighter in colour, also taller and more refined in bearing. G. Forster, in his exaggerated manner, imagines that these nobles are so far ahead of the ordinary man as to appear an entirely different type of human. Yet, he expressly emphasises the relation between a lighter skin and delicate features with a more comfortable, inactive mode of life. But he found in the mind and character of these individuals a certain refinement, if not a certain nobility. The nobles, being both chieftains and priests, were also the will-power and the intelligentsia of Polynesia, with a monopoly of knowledge and of philosophy based on knowledge." [3] Such is Ratzel's view of this question.

Different classes may assume the character of different races. On the other hand, the meeting of many races, each developing an occupation of its own, may lead to their taking up various callings or social positions within the same community; race becomes class. Particularly frequent is the case of a poor but warlike nomadic race at-

[3] Ratzel, *op. cit.*, vol. ii, pp. 590, 591.

tacking a prosperous, peaceful peasant population and subjecting it, the former race then assuming the function of a warrior nobility with a monopoly of national defence. This nobility will develop exclusively warlike properties, despise productive labour, and the workers will become poor, badly nourished, defenceless, and unmilitant, which qualities may, in some cases, develop to the point of cowardice.

When race traits coincide with vocational traits, they are further sharpened and intensified by the division of labour.

On the other hand, the intensification of a property acquired in vocational life or class life into a race trait may be encouraged by the fact that the members of a class or of a calling are forced to marry only within their own group. This may be in part a consequence of the arrogance of the upper class, which despises the other classes, but it may also result from reasons of selection: the ruling class wishes to preserve undiminished its predominant qualities, by which it has obtained power, and therefore seeks to avoid any mingling with other groups, lacking in such qualities. The heredity of the traits of the dominant class must be rendered safe. On the other hand, groups that have been depressed to the lowest level are prohibited from mingling with the rest of the population, in order that the latter may not be contaminated with the defects of these outcasts.

As in the case of domestic animals it is also sought to

conserve predominant traits among the classes by maintaining the race "pure". But man is not a domestic animal, and purity of race encounters many difficulties in the human existence.

It is not sufficient, in the case of domestic animals, that the stud-animals be preserved from breeding with foreign species. Even among these race animals, it is always the best specimens that are chosen and used as reproducing animals. The others, less excellent, are often destroyed and always excluded from reproduction.

But no class among humans may proceed so harshly toward its own members, no matter how far superior the class interest may appear in its eyes to that of the individual. A class often arrogates to itself, or bestows upon the child's father, the right to decide whether the child is to be brought up or killed. The Christian order of Teutonic Knights were freed from the necessity of making this choice by their opportunity to put into a monastery weak or unwarlike boys, and thus prevent them from producing legitimate offspring. But these methods of selection were not always applied in accordance with considerations of breeding only, often being crossed by other considerations. A father desiring an heir, and not having obtained one that was healthy, probably did not kill his weak child, but brought him up, and instead of condemning him to celibacy may even have married him off.

In order to preserve the race pure as a class, it is necessary to have complete control of the sexual life of woman

—not of man. The man's illegitimate offspring do not become members of the ruling class, but adultery on the part of the legitimate wife, unless discovered, impairs the purity of the race. The freer woman is, the easier it will be for her to commit adultery. Lack of freedom for the woman, when it goes so far as to shut her up in a harem, like a cow in a stable, is always associated with polygamy, but since the number of women everywhere is about equal to that of men, it implies that women not belonging to the ruling class may be elevated to the status of wife. Furthermore, even the woman in the harem is by no means a cow in a stable and completely deprived of her freedom of action. Even such a woman may find opportunities for adultery, as was already observed by the Sultan Scheherban, who said there was only one means of assuring oneself of a woman's fidelity: killing her after the first embrace.

If, in spite of all these obstacles, the purity of a race is maintained intact, further misfortune threatens from inbreeding. Inbreeding may remain harmless for long periods, when only healthy individuals are chosen for reproduction. The exploiting class, which has consolidated its power and controls great wealth, is, however, likely to yield to a life of idle enjoyment, with its degenerating results. When this is the case, inbreeding still further accentuates decay, and it does this the more, the purer the race.

We thus find that the phenomenon of race is far more

complicated in man than in the animal world. The sharpness of race demarcation, which is evident in the case of animals, disappears more and more among men. In the place of sharply distinct races, unchanged for long periods, we find a constant and increasingly rapid process of race disintegration; the formation of new races, race mixtures, conditioned by the general process of technical, economic, social evolution, arising from this process and closely interlaced with it. It becomes more and more difficult to distinguish between inherited properties and those acquired by the individual; races become more manifold, also the race traits, more and more varied are the individuals within each human group, more and more variable and important become the extremely changeable mental traits, instead of the less easily changing somatic traits; these mental traits cannot be completely defined by any measurement, and may often be inferred only from the most fugitive observations.

There is probably no more difficult task than that of observing the influence of race, as an isolated factor, in any specific phenomenon of human history. The task becomes the more difficult and—at least for our present ways and means of investigation—more hopeless, the more we advance in history, the more the races mingle, the more varied and powerful become the artificial conditions under which they live.

Our race theoreticians regard that which is perhaps the most complicated problem in human history as the simple and self-evident explanation of this history. The concept of race, extremely fluctuating even in the case of animal and vegetable organisms, where it is not complicated, is regarded by them as a firm basis upon which the entire theory and practice of human society may be built up without hesitation.

CHAPTER IV

DIFFERENCES AND OPPOSITIONS BETWEEN THE RACES OF MAN

WHILE the literary and journalistic race theoreticians regard the concept of race in the case of man as something self-evident, natural scientists are by no means agreed on the division of human races, but are obliged to admit that everything is in a state of flux. Darwin tells us:

"Our naturalist would likewise be much disturbed as soon as he should discern that the distinctive traits of man are extremely variable. . . . We may doubt whether any trait may be adduced that is distinctive and constant for a certain race. . . . The form of the skull varies considerably in certain races; likewise every other trait. . . . The races of man graduate into each other, independently, in many cases, as far as we can judge, of their having intercrossed. Man has been studied more thoroughly than any other organic being, and yet there is the greatest possible diversity amongst capable judges whether he should be classed as a single species or race, or as two (Virey), as three (Jacquinot), as four (Kant), five (Blumenbach), six (Buffon), seven (Hunter), eight (Agassiz), eleven (Pickering), fifteen (Bory St. Vincent), sixteen (Desmoulins), twenty-two (Morton), sixty (Crawfurd), or sixty-three (Burke)." [1]

These words were written half a century ago, but are just as applicable today. In their embarrassment, many anthropologists finally resort to the device of classifying a series of races not by their somatic traits, but by *language*, concerning which Ernst Häckel maintains with a straight face that it "is transmitted far more rigidly than the skull forms".[2]

Of course, the only thing inherited is the ability to speak, not the specific language. Language is acquired, the earliest and most important teachers being the persons among whom the individual grows up when a child, not necessarily the parents in every case. Owing to migrations, to altered environment, to contacts with strange peoples, the ancestral language may be forgotten, and a foreign language acquired, while the native pigmentation of hair, eyes, skin, the form of the nose, etc., are not lost. Any races may, without in any way changing their ·acial character, change their language and, *vice versa*, the most different races may appear in succession in a certain region, each supplanting the other, and each receiving its language from its predecessors. In present-day Greece, practically the same Greek language is spoken as two or three thousand years ago, and yet, how many races have succeeded each

---

[1] Charles Darwin, *The Descent of Man*, London, 1871, vol. ii, pp. 225, 226.

[2] *Natürliche Schöpfungsgeschichte*, 5th ed., p. 602.

other in that country! On the other hand, the Irish have abandoned their Celtic language in the course of the last few centuries, without noticeably changing their "race". If language were a race trait, the Negroes of the United States would have to be counted as Anglo-Saxons, and many Negroes and Indians of Central and South America as Latins. In fact, some Negroes would also have to be classified as Germans. A German scientist was much surprised to encounter, in the primeval Brazilian forest, a Negro who spoke Low German. His master was a colonist who had immigrated to Brazil from the *Waterkant*, a part of Germany where Low German is spoken.

As a matter of fact, language is even less an indication of race than skin, hair, or head-form. There is no Semitic race, there is no Aryan race. The Aryan race is not a primitive race, but merely an "invention of the closeted scholar." [3]

This does not mean that language may not be of great importance in defining the groups of mankind. Language is their means of communication, of social cooperation. When men speak the same language, it is easy for them to live and work together. When brought together by the material conditions of life and labour, they must seek to make themselves understood by each other by means of a common language. Thus, language is in a state of constant and close interaction with the compass of this social grouping of men; it becomes one of the most important

[3] Dr. E. Houzé, *L'Aryen et l'anthropologie*, Brussels, 1906, p. 33.

means of uniting and segregating men; and the study of old linguistic survivals may at times help us in reconstructing the history of social groupings in periods that afford no other evidence on this point. It is no doubt justifiable to divide mankind according to language groups, but this division by no means coincides with the division according to race. Originally, while each race of man represented a geographical race, a human group inhabiting certain regions for many thousands of years, under like conditions, each race may also have developed a type of language peculiar to itself, a language dividing off into many dialects. A common language tree points in the first place to a former common home, and to the common life conditions of this home, and, in very primitive peoples, to membership in the same geographical race. But there is probably not a single tribe today that inhabits the primitive seats in which the language now spoken by this tribe was formed, without any mixture with other tribes. The more varied its wanderings, its mingling with other races, its historical destinies, the more will language and race become independent of each other. And, as the means of intercourse grow, as the groups of men become larger and larger who are united by their economy in permanent social cooperation, the sooner will very different races and race mixtures be embraced in a single linguistic and cultural group. On the other hand, this same increase in the means of intercourse, as the members of the same race are drawn into the most different regions of the earth, attaching them to the most different human communities, must divide many races into a number of linguistically different sections, so that many descendants of the same race will understand each other less and less, will become mentally less and less connected with each other.

Language as a race trait is therefore of no value.

And modern anthropologists are of quite different opinion on the matter of race from those "anthropo-sociologists" who term themselves thus because they know as little of anthropology as of sociology. Professor Felix von Luschan, of Berlin, presented a very interesting outline of the "anthropological view of race" at the First General Racial Congress held in London in 1911. We are giving his remarks in some detail, including those in which excellent light is thrown upon the pseudo-scientific race-conceit of our colonial fanatics of the Rohrbach type. Luschan said, among other things:

"Coloured people are often described as savage races, but it is comparatively rare to find any attempts to give a proper definition of *coloured* and *savage*.

"A certain order issued by a European governor in Africa once stated what Negroes, Arabs, Hindus, Portuguese, Greeks, and other coloured people had to do on meeting a white man, and in the German Reichstag one of the successors of Bismarck once spoke of the Samoans as a 'handful of savages'. Again, many books have been written on the differences between races of men, and serious scientists have tried in vain to draw up an exact definition of what really constitutes the difference between savage and civilised races. It is very easy to speak of 'Greeks and other coloured people'; but some assign the ancient Greeks to the civilised races, and are so severe in their division as to exclude from that group the ancient Romans as half-barbarians.

"The division of mankind into active and passive races is an old one. Since then an attempt was made to put 'twilight' races between the 'day' races and the 'night' races, and the Japanese were included in this group of *Dämmerungsmenschen,*—the Japanese, who are now in the van of human civilisation in Asia, and who have, perhaps, saved the mental freedom of Europe at Tsushima and on the battlefields of Manchuria.

"Still weaker and more objectionable is the division as to colour. We now know that colour of hair and skin is only the effect of environment, and that we are fair only because our ancestors lived for thousands, or probably tens of thousands, of years in sunless and foggy countries. Fairness is nothing else but lack of pigment, and our ancestors lost part of their pigment because they did not need it. Just as the *Proteus sanguineus* and certain beetles became blind in caves, where their eyes were useless, so we poor fair people have to wear dark glasses and gloves when walking on a glacier, and get our skin burned when we expose it unduly to the light of the sun.

"It is therefore only natural that certain Indian races and the Singhalese are dark; but it would be absurd to call

69

them 'savage' on that account, as they have an ancient civilisation, and had a noble and refined religion at a time when our own ancestors had a very low standard of life." [4]

With the aid of many examples, Luschan then shows that the alleged inferiority of savages is in many cases only an apparent inferiority, the proofs adduced in favour of this inferiority being often merely a consequence of the simplicity and impatience of their observers, who inferred the absence of intelligence where intelligence was absent only from the observers. Luschan continues, in the same paper from which we have already quoted:

"In former times it was not so much the mental and material culture of foreign races as their anatomical qualities, which were taken as the starting point, in showing their inferiority. Especially in America, before the Civil War, anthropology (or what they called by that name) was engaged in showing that the Negro, with his black skin, his prognathism, his blubber-lips and his short and broad nose, was no real human being but a domestic animal. How to treat him was the owner's private affair; it was nobody else's business, any more than the treatment of his cattle or horses.

"Even today there are scientists who claim a separate origin for the various human types, and who link one palæolithic race to the Gorilla and another to the Orang.

---

[4] *Anthropological View of Race*, reprinted in *Papers on Inter-racial Problems, Communicated to the First Universal Races Congress, held at the University of London, July 26-29*, pp. 13 *et seq.*

DIFFERENCES AND OPPOSITIONS

The author of *Anthropozoon biblicum* goes still further and wants us to believe that the dark races are the descendants of incestuous intercourse between 'Aryans' and monkeys. But the great majority of our modern authorities now claim a monogenetic origin for all of mankind.

"So the question of the number of human races has quite lost its *raison d'être*, and has become a subject rather of philosophical speculation than of scientific research. It is of no more importance now to know how many human races there are than to know how many angels can dance on the point of a needle. Our aim now is to find out how ancient and primitive races developed from others, and how races have changed or evolved through migration or interbreeding.

"We do not yet know where the first man began to develop from earlier stages of zoological existence. . . . We shall probably not be far from the truth if we say that the palæolithic man of Europe was not essentially different from the modern Australian. If we are allowed to draw conclusions as to the soft parts from the parts of the skeleton, our palæolithic ancestor had dark skin, dark eyes, and dark, more or less, straight hair. His home was probably in some part of Southern Asia; but we find similar types even now among the Toala of Celebes and the Veddas of Ceylon. In fact, millions of dark men in India belong to the same stock, and so do all the dark tribes of Afghanistan and Beluchistan.

ARE THE JEWS A RACE?

"So we can trace an early and primitive type of mankind from Gibraltar, Moustier, Spy, Neandertal, Kropina, etc., to Ceylon, Celebes, and Australia. This certainly is a wide area, but every year is now bringing fresh proofs of this direct continuity of a distinct human type from the earliest palæolithic ages to modern times.

"The question naturally arises how it is that our Australian brothers have remained for fifty or a hundred thousand years, or longer, in such a primitive state of mental and material culture, while we Europeans have reached the height of modern civilisation. The answer is not difficult. Australia was isolated from the rest of the world through an early geological catastrophe soon after the immigration of palæolithic man. Every impulse and incentive from without ceased, and human life began to petrify.

"It was quite otherwise in Europe and in Western Asia. The thousand advantages of the environment, the broken coastlines, the many islands, the navigable rivers, and especially the constant passing from Asia to Europe and from Europe to Asia and Africa, the ready exchange of inventions and discoveries and acquisitions, the incessant trade and traffic, have made us what we are.

"This primitive but uniform human type began to change chiefly in two directions. To the southwest of the line connecting Gibraltar with Australia, man, in some way or other, developed curly and woolly hair, and so became what we now call Protonigritian. We find his descendants

72

in Melanesia and in Africa. The Pygmies form a very old branch of this protonigritic group. . . .

"On the other side of this line, in Northern Asia, primitive man acquired, during many thousands of years, straight hair and a shorter or broader skull. The modern Chinese, and the typical, now nearly extinct, American Indians, are at the end of this northeastern line of development, while the typical Negro represents the southwestern end.

"We have thus three chief varieties of mankind—the old Indo-European, the African, and the East-Asiatic, all branching off from the same primitive stock, diverging from each other for thousands, perhaps hundreds of thousands, of years, but all these forming *a complete unity, intermarrying in all directions without the slightest decrease in fertility.*

"From these three varieties came all the different types of modern mankind, generally by local isolation. A very interesting example of such mutation is found in the earliest known inhabitants of Western Asia. This is the land of those extremely narrow and high-arched noses, we generally call Jewish or even Semitic. These remarkable noses, however, do not belong to the Semitic invaders, of whom Abraham is the eponymic hero, but to the pre-Semitic population which might be called Hittite or Armenoid, as the modern Armenians are their direct descendants.

"These old Hittites or Armenoids emigrated in very

early times to Europe, where the 'Alpine Race' descended from them. In the most out-of-the-way valleys of Savoy, Graubünden, Tyrol, and Carinthia, more than half of the population has the head-form and the nose of this second immigration from Asia to Europe, and from the mingling of this short-headed 'Alpine Race' with the descendants of the long-headed Palæolithic or Neanderthal or proto-Australian Race, all the great modern European races have sprung. . . .

"While the first varieties of primitive man were certainly formed *and fixed* by long isolation, later variations were caused by migration and colonisation. . . .

"In former times ethnologists used to admire the apparent unity in the direction of the human mind, and to wonder how it was that in all parts of the earth men had similar ideas and ways. Now this *Völkergedanken* theory is nearly abandoned, and we are forced to admit the real unity of mankind. Fair and dark races, long- and short-headed, intelligent and primitive, all come from one stock. Favourable circumstances and surroundings, especially a good environment, a favourable geographical position, trade and traffic, caused one group to advance more quickly than another, while some groups have remained in a very primitive state of development, but all are adapted to their surroundings, according to the law of the survival of the fittest."

This mode of thought can hardly be better characterised than in the words of Luschan, and we have therefore given

74

them in full. Essentially, this is the attitude of all of modern anthropology; of course, the various scientists differ considerably as to matters of detail, but this does not alter their essential agreement.

But we shall not take up this subject here. The important point is that modern anthropology does not consider differences of race to be an impassible gulf. The races are in a state of constant flux and transition, all are of the same origin in the long run; none of the dominant races may boast that its present superiority is based on its blood and is immutable so long as the race preserves its purity. We may not maintain that any of the subject races owes its servitude to a natural immutable inferiority. The superiority of one group is to be ascribed only to favourable circumstances in the environment, the backwardness of the other group to unfavourable circumstances. We may say of any race that under the same favourable circumstances it will accomplish as much as the highest races—not necessarily, however, at once. The Teutons mentioned by Tacitus lived about one hundred and fifty years after those mentioned by Cæsar, and seem to have remained just as barbarous as the latter. Fully ten centuries were required, after the Teutonic migrations, before society again attained the level of the defunct Græco-Roman civilisation, and further centuries have intervened before the attainment of our present level of civilisation. It is sometimes carelessly denied that Negroes have any cultural aptitude because in the United States, in the sixty years that have elapsed since their liberation, they have not yet so far emerged from the state of barbarism in which they had lived before their liberation, as to produce a Darwin or a Kant. And yet, the Negroes in the United States are methodically kept in a state of the greatest ignorance, having great difficulty even in obtaining such necessary and "inalienable" rights as the most rudimentary schooling.

Only a few years after the liberation of the Negroes, Häckel considered it his privilege to write: "The *ulotriches* (woolly-haired) are incapable of any true inner culture or of a higher mental training, even under such favourable (?) conditions of adaptation as have now been offered them in the United States of America." [5]

A fine view for an "evolutionist" to hold! Truly, Häckel has no ground for this view, which is being relinquished more and more by anthropologists, except where the demands of a "scientific" pretext for a colonial policy revive such prejudices.

One thing is no doubt true: the leading races of modern civilisation have advanced with such immense rapidity in the last few centuries, particularly in their technology, that their lead has become more and more extensive, leaving the backward peoples farther and farther behind along the path the latter must follow in order to attain the level of the civilised races. But this by no means signifies that the backward peoples will and must continue to re-

[5] Ernst Häckel, *Natürliche Schöpfungsgeschichte*, 5th ed., p. 603.

main backward. The rapid progress of the European nations since the Sixteenth Century was due only to an expansion of trade which brought all the races and peoples of the earth into the closest contact with each other. The first effect of this process was to destroy the weakest races, for modern society is based on brutal hostilities of interests: it destroyed them body and soul. Some were exterminated, forced down into the status of domestic animals and doomed to the stupidity of the latter—like the present condition of the European proletarians. But this tendency did not everywhere have a permanently degrading effect. As in the case of all the more energetic strata of the proletariat, there will also come a time for the more energetic of the backward races subjugated by capitalism, when their degradation will lead them to rebel against this degradation and thus proceed along an upward course. This rise can only be accomplished by taking possession of the mental and material weapons by which the "master races" have created their dominant position. The handicap of the dominant capitalist nations is too great for any one of the oppressed nations to believe that they may overcome it by self-devised means. They hasten to follow the lead of the "more civilised" and are gradually catching up with them by means of the processes devised and prepared by the leading nations themselves. The backward nations are spared the necessity of this labour of seeking and trail-blazing, and they may thus accomplish in a few decades that which required many centuries on the part of the leading nations. Of course, in order to achieve this, they must relinquish their originality, their original native traits, their spiritual independence.

Man's teeth have suffered owing to the cooking and the artificial dividing of foodstuffs. His memory has very probably suffered owing to his use of writing and printing. Similarly, the inventive spirit of the backward peoples is probably being much weakened by their acquisition of so many superior inventions ready-made, requiring the use of their full mental powers to absorb them. The greater half of mankind is transformed from intelligently investigating creatures into imitative creatures, into mere pupils of superior teachers.

But this also is merely a transient stage, from which each people emerges as soon as it has attained the level of modern civilisation, after which it begins to partake actively in this civilisation.

The permanent result of this process of development must finally be a mental similarity of the human race, on the basis of this civilisation, in which the already very variable and indefinite mental race traits will be far more quickly eradicated than bodily traits, in order to be absorbed in a new body of traits, within which other, greater, individual differences will arise. Types disappear, individualities grow. The point of departure in human evolution was probably a uniform human race. This race is divided into an increasing number of races, which is now again forming a new community of the human race, but a community of a different kind. Ratzel, in his *Anthropogeographie*, has already mentioned this process, which, like his "negation" and his "negation of negation", is a dialectic process resembling that expounded by Marx in *Capital*, there ending with the expropriation of the expropriators. Ratzel's words, taken from the book above mentioned, are as follows:

"The similarity of species in present-day mankind is of far different origin than the similarities between the various animal and plant species. The latter similarities are caused by a more and more emphatic development of specific traits in a certain definite direction, while mankind has become more and more a unit—and will become even more so— by the combination of its formerly far diverging groups. These two groups of similarities have therefore come into being by entirely different paths, the former by segregation, the latter by conjoining and combining. Therefore the former are more limited in area, while the latter embrace the entire earth. And therefore these similarities are of different character also. The closed system of animal and plant species may be contrasted with the varied character of the branches of mankind, which are based on a great mass of reduced or attenuated differences which, however, tend more and more to combine, to make mankind a more unified mass. Present-day humanity may be conceived as standing, in time, midway between a humanity of the past, with greater internal differences, perhaps even differences of species, and a humanity of the future, with much smaller internal differences." [6]

Ratzel is here concerned chiefly with the effects of race mixture. Like most anthropologists, he does not pay sufficient attention to the economic factor. But he is well aware of the tendency of evolution, and also of the differences between the race development of animals and that of historical man. The future belongs not to a separation of races into exploiting and exploited, or—as it is sometimes put more euphemistically—into active and passive, into day races and night races, but to a dissolving of races in a single human race. The first step in this direction will be a mental combination, an economic equality, from which there must result an increasing "toning down or attenuation of differences"—even though esthetes may turn up their noses at this possibility.

Of course, Werner Sombart is one of these esthetes. He considers it imperative to maintain the race differences existing between men, for: "Who would want to miss the racy Judiths and Miriams? To be sure, they must be racy and ready to remain so. We cannot tolerate this black-blond mix-up." [7]

And since "we" do not desire any diminution of race traits, the historical process will respectfully refrain from touching them. In this connection, Sombart had already forgotten in 1912 what he was still aware of in 1911,

[6] Vol. ii, p. 585.
[7] Die Zukunft der Juden, Leipzig, 1912, p. 72.

namely, "That when I say: this woman is *racy* (has *class*), this does not mean the same as when I say: this person belongs to the Mongolian *race*." [8]

Anthropologists and scientific students in general speak of the Mongolian race; but the concept of a "racy" woman is born in those learned circles whose chief interest centres about horses and women of a certain class, to whom it transfers the jargon of the stable.

In spite of all these esthetic individuals, the attenuation of the races can hardly be retarded. Capitalism is working with all its might in this development and thus preparing a higher form of society by this means also. To socialism falls the task of strengthening the oppressed and disinherited against the exploitation of capitalism, of leading them to the victory, in other words, of making them not only superior in strength to their exploiters, but also of making them their superiors or at least their equals in mental maturity.

The result of all this conflict and struggle between the capitalists and the proletarians of the advanced nations and the rebellious strata of the backward nations, is not only the international solidarity of the proletariat of the civilised nations, but—in the last analysis—the international unity of the entire human race in thought and knowledge, in investigation and aspirations.

Finally we shall behold the realisation of the dictum first uttered as an ideal of the thinkers and pioneers of the

[8] *Die Juden und das Wirtschaftsleben,* Leipzig, 1911, p. 349.

revolutionary bourgeoisie, the dictum adopted ready-made by the revolutionary proletariat:

Alle Menschen, gleich geboren,
Sind ein adliges Geschlecht.

This aspiration might still have been considered chimerical some years ago. But in the meantime, the victories of the Japanese over Russia have revealed to all the world the extent to which Asia has been revolutionised by capitalism and by the uprisings of its nations. These nations, of whom it was once assumed that their conservative adherence to the traditional forms of life was of their very essence—of the marrow of their bones, as it were, a permanent race trait—have now become a revolutionary element in world history.

Not only the victory of the proletariat of the white races, but also the liberation of the "coloured" races, is only a question of time.

But is not this struggle for liberation a race struggle? Is it not a portion of the uninterrupted struggle of the races which has been going on from time immemorial and which must continue to be waged because the struggle for existence is a natural necessity?

We have seen that the struggle for existence in the animal world is almost exclusively a struggle against surrounding nature, not against individuals of the same species. In nature, this struggle—as a rule—is not even a struggle between different varieties of the same species. For these varieties are geographical in their origin, each having its special territory, within which it lives in a condition of equilibrium, and which it does not leave unless this equilibrium is disturbed, an event therefore traceable to geological eras.

In the case of man the situation changes. Man's technology destroys the equilibrium in nature and also the equilibrium in his own ranks. In many regions we now find overpopulation ensuing, combined with a struggle for food resources. But this is not a struggle of race against race, but rather at first a struggle waged by the horde against a neighbouring horde which seeks to displace it, when all sources of food have been cut off. This cannot be called a race struggle, but a struggle within the race. The hordes and tribes were far too small to enable us to consider any single one of them as an entire race; each was but a portion of the same race.

If this condition of overpopulation continues, the movement will probably involve all the tribes of a certain region, some of whom must immigrate. These may advance so far as to come into hostile contact with hordes or tribes of another race, but the struggle with these groups is at bottom no different from that within the same race. At most, the foreign appearance of the opponent may accentuate the ruthlessness of the struggle and the completeness of the victory. But even here the differences in language and culture, making a mutual understanding difficult, are of greater effect than the differences in race traits.

As civilisation advances, the social groups develop into states and nations; but even these are by no means synonymous with races. We have the simultaneous development of the differences between classes and of the oppositions between exploiters and exploited. These oppositions are a determining element not only in the internal, but also in the external politics of states. The exploiters seek to increase the number of those exploited by them, in order to increase the profits of exploitation, either by seizures of men, by slavery, or by the conquest of new regions and by the subjection of their inhabitants. The cause for war is no longer overpopulation, but exploitation: struggles between exploiters and exploited, or between the exploiters among themselves for the ownership of an exploited community.

The deep roots of these struggles are not to be found in the differences of race, but in the social conditions. It is possible that the opposing groups of those interested may be of different races, but this is by no means the rule, for it is self-evident that the first persons with whom one comes in contact either as exploiter or as one exploited are one's own neighbours. It was quite a common thing to find Greek and Italian slaves among the ancient Athenians and Romans, while Negro slaves were practically unknown. The relation of exploitation, the opposition of interests, does not arise from differences of race, which may only serve as a contributing cause for rendering the expressions of this opposition more brutal.

Even in cases where opposing interested groups belong to different races and, differing even in their external earmarks, are brought into savage opposition to each other, we never find a race unified in its conflict with another. We are always dealing with individual groups, each of which may enter into the most varied combinations with other groups either of its own race or of another race.

Many of the Negro slaves brought by white traders to America had formerly been the slaves of other Negroes who had sold them to the whites.

The struggle between Indians and "palefaces" in North America may appear to have been a race struggle. But the whites, after their arrival in America, did not act as representatives of one and the same race, cooperating with each other, but as the representatives of different states, fighting each other bitterly. In this struggle, each sought and obtained the assistance of Indian tribes. During the entire Eighteenth Century, we find whites struggling against whites in America; Frenchmen against Englishmen, later American colonials against Englishmen, and Indians against Indians. And where we find Indians fighting the whites, they were often acting on the instigation of other whites.

But it is sufficient to consider our own epoch, in which the conception of the race struggle plays such an important part, to reveal the emptiness and ridiculousness of this phrase.

ARE THE JEWS A RACE?

We are told that the "race" of the Teutons is destined by nature for a life-and-death struggle with the "race" of the Slavs and the Romance races. It was found necessary to increase the German army because the Balkan War had disturbed the equilibrium between Teutons and Slavs and Austria was now threatened by the Southern Slavs. But it was not the race of the Teutons that had come into hostile contact with the Europeans, but the more or less impure race of landed proprietors (agrarians), particularly the Hungarian, Polish and Bohemian junkers, who cared mighty little about the Teutonic race!

But simultaneously the Teutons of Germany, in order to wage the "race" struggle against the Latins of France, allied themselves with the Latins of Italy. For a time, our Teutons also aimed to obtain the friendship of the Teutonic race in England; then, "blood was thicker than water". But later, the English Teutons wickedly sought an entente with Russia, the home of the Slavic race, and with the principal Romance race, France, in order to oppose their Teutonic blood-kindred in Germany!

Like the "Aryan" and "Semitic", the Teutonic or the Slavic race, the race struggle itself is an invention of the brains of schoolmasters, rejected by serious scholars.

This was the case even before the World War, which forced the German Government to seek the aid of the Turks and of the entire Mohammedan world, while, during the war, France and England, and later America, sent coloured regiments against their white enemies. This

86

would appear to be a peculiar phase of the race struggle. Eduard Meyer once said concerning this struggle:

"While the differences in somatic structure, and particularly of skin pigment, have always been obvious, they have never had any effect on the relations between nations except where these sharp distinctions involved not only mere external appearance, but also—and particularly— a difference in the cultural aptitude and the mode of thought, as between Europeans and Negroes. In this field also, it was reserved for our time to assign an inner significance to the external contrast, and many theories, in their far-fetched application, have ascribed to the factor of race a significance which it never possessed and which is in direct contradiction with all the experiences of history.

"The popular notion that the hostility to the Jews ('anti-Semitism') is a race hostility, or that it has anything to do with race, is completely erroneous; we find this hostility among the closest of kin to the Jews, as well as among the Europeans. It is generally known that the importance of race is hardly dreamed of in the Orient and that even the aversion for the Negro is found fully developed only among the Teutonic (English) tribes." [9]

There is surely nothing more absurd than the theory of the "natural" hostility between races, but unfortunately it is not one of the theories that may be killed by laughing at it. It arises from interests that are too strong, it serves too well the purpose of facilitating the demagogic exploita-

[9] Eduard Meyer, *Geschichte des Altertums*, I, 1, 3rd ed., 1910, p. 77.

tion of ancient prejudices and errors on the subject of foreign phenomena, to prevent this absurd creature of the overheated pedantic brain to be considered in editorial offices and on the parliamentary rostrum, by professional patriots as a recognised science, as a self-evident truth, imparting to it ever new accessions of vitality.

CHAPTER V

PHYSICAL CHARACTERISTICS OF THE JEWISH RACE

We have seen that the traits derived from the primitive races of man tend more and more to disappear, as the economic evolution progresses. Race mixtures and a constant transformation in the economic conditions are ceaselessly at work on the creation of new types, again subject to progressive change, in part to new differentiations, in part to new combinations, causing a continual weakening of the definiteness and permanence of races, and also bringing about more and more variety in individual differentiation. The process of history is not a continuous struggle between immutable races, but a process of uninterrupted alteration in the economic environment, of constant change in the groups of interests struggling with each other, resulting in a constant mutation in the traditional race traits as determined by the original state of nature. Race, meaning the races of animals—wild animals as well as domestic animals—becomes more and more vague among men, departing further and further from the divisions of men into states and languages, as developed in the course of historical evolution.

ARE THE JEWS A RACE?

It may therefore be assumed in advance, in the case of a group of humans that have marched for tens of centuries in the front rank of the process of economic evolution, that have undergone the most extensive migrations, economic and political revolutions, that there is no possibility that such a race may be a unit or a pure race.

But we are told this statement does not apply to the Jews. It is claimed, again and again, that the Jewish race has maintained itself in all its purity since time immemorial, and this alleged permanence of the Jewish racial type has become one of the most frequently utilised bases of the views of race theory among the anthropo-sociologists.

A full century ago, Blumenbach wrote: "It is generally known that the Jewish race has been spread for many centuries over all the earth; it has nevertheless maintained its racial traits pure and even typical. This remarkable fact has long been receiving the attention of scientists and physiologists."

The well-known anthropologist, Richard Andree, declared:

"Anthropologically considered, the Jews are one of the most interesting subjects. For no other race type can be traced back through tens of centuries *with the same certainty* as the Jews, and no other race type presents such permanent forms, no other has so well resisted the influence of time and the influence of its environment." [1]

This view is widely accepted to this day as an irrefutable

[1] Quoted by Fishberg, p. 9.

and unquestionable fact, a fact which is so irrefutable and unquestionable that its advocate forgets to state what are the appallingly constant and immutable traits of the Jewish race. The race theorists usually hand over this scientific task to the cartoonists of the comic papers.

These most dependable scholars have found the principal trait of Judaism in its nose. The comic papers picture no Jew without the Jewish nose. But what is the state of affairs outside of the comic papers?

Fishberg states:

"The present author has investigated the subject among Jews in New York City and also in the various countries east and west of Europe, in North Africa, and Jewish immigrants of various countries in Asia. The results of these investigations do not bear out the popular notion that the hooked nose is to be considered the 'Jewish' nose, because only a small minority of Jews have the privilege of possessing this kind of nose. Among 2,836 adult male Jews in New York City, the percentage of noses was as follows:

> Straight, or Greek.................57.26%
> Retroussé, or Snub 22.07%
> Aquiline, or Hooked 14.25%
> Flat and Broad 6.42%

Among 1,284 Jewesses, the percentage of straight noses was even higher, and of aquiline and hooked noses even smaller than among the men:

Straight, or Greek 59.42%
Retroussé, or Snub 13.86%
Aquiline, or Hooked 12.70%
Flat and Broad ....14.02%" [2]

But a small portion of the Jews, therefore—thirteen or fourteen per cent.—have the Jewish nose!

Fishberg is not the only investigator who has found this percentage so low. Other scholars working in Russia and Austria have arrived at the same result.

On the other hand, we find that the aquiline nose is by no means possessed by Jews only. It is quite common in Western Asia, on the Mediterranean Sea, as well as among American Indians. We have already quoted Luschan's observation that the Jewish nose is particularly frequent in the Alpine valleys that are cut off from all outside influences, that it is an earmark of the *homo alpinus*, the Alpine man. While but thirteen or fourteen per cent. of the Jews have a Jewish nose—as a rule—the conservative Catholic population of Ancient Bavaria* shows thirty-one per cent. of Jewish noses.

A further observation of Fishberg's is very interesting: the forms of noses found among Jews have a tendency to vary with the forms of noses in the environment in which they live.

"It is noteworthy that Bavarian Jews also have a higher

[2] Fishberg, p. 79.
* *Altbayern,* former designation for the Bavarian provinces of Upper and Lower Bavaria.—TRANSLATOR.

proportion of hooked noses than their co-religionists in other countries." [3]

Wide noses are found more frequently among the Jews of Northern Africa than among those of Eastern Europe. But the snub nose, on the other hand, among Jews, is most numerous among those living in the midst of a Slavic population, where this type of nose, as is well known, is very frequent.

If we are obliged to relinquish the Jewish nose, we are giving up the most widely recognised race trait of the Jews. What other such traits do we still have? Skin pigmentation, eye pigmentation, hair pigmentation? These are often mentioned as race traits, but if we are to consider black hair, dark eyes, swarthy or sallow skin as particular traits of the Jews, we should have to regard as Jews all Europeans that are not blond.

Furthermore, there are blond and blue-eyed persons among the Jews. Among 4,235 Jews examined by Fishberg in New York, the following were the proportions:

	Jews	Jewesses
Brunette Type	52.62%	56.94%
Blond Type	10.42%	10.27%
Mixed Types	36.96%	32.79%

"The brunette type, which is considered characteristic of the Jews from time immemorial, is thus reduced to only fifty-two per cent. among the European representatives of

[3] Fishberg, p. 83.

the race, while among the Jewesses it is not much larger, fifty-seven per cent." [4]

But the blond Jew is not equally numerous everywhere:

"On the whole, it can be stated that most of the blond Jews are found in countries where the general population has a considerable proportion of blonds. This is exemplified by the number of blond Jews in England, twenty-five per cent., and in Germany, where over thirty per cent. of Jewish children had blond hair. On the other hand, in Italy, where the Christian population is distinctly brunette, less than five per cent. of the Jews are blond, while in Algeria, Bokhara, the Caucasus, etc., the percentage is even less." [5]

We have still to consider the skull. The skull is said to be an unchanging race trait. Where the race has been preserved in its purity, the skull, according to many anthropologists, will not change, while others dispute this condition. This is not the place to attempt the solution of such controversies. Assuming that the form of the skull is the decisive factor, by which we mean whether the form of the skull, as viewed from above, shows a greater or less ratio between length and breadth, what are the results that may be said to have been determined by skull measurements?

"It may, in fact, be stated that there is no single type of head which is found among the Jews of all countries in

[4] Fishberg, p. 66.
[5] Fishberg, p. 70.

94

which they live. Indeed nearly all varieties of skulls are met with among Jews of today." [6]

The head-forms of the Jews in various countries are quite different from each other. The condition is as follows:

	Daghestan, Caucasus	Jews in Europe	North Africa	Yemen, Arabia
Hyperdolichocephalic (−76)..	....	2.89%	25.97%	71.80%
Dolichocephalic (76-77)	....	7.36	24.67	14.10
Subdolichocephalic (78-79)....	4.70%	15.51	19.48	7.69
Mesocephalic (80-81)	6.10	25.78	13.00	2.56
Subbrachycephalic (82-83) ...	17.37	24.01	9.09	3.85
Brachycephalic (84-85)	23.94	15.97	6.49	....
Hyperbrachycephalic (86+)...	47.89	8.47	1.30	....
Number of Observations	213	2,641	77	78 [7]

The Jews in the Caucasus are therefore predominantly brachycephalic, while those in Northern Africa, and particularly those in Arabia, are predominantly dolichocephalic, and those in Europe predominantly of medium types.

Fishberg therefore rightly observes:

"As far as head-form is concerned, these three groups of Jews represent three different races as clearly as if they were of white, black, and yellow skin." [8]

---

[6] Fishberg, p. 49.

[7] These figures (the cephalic index) indicate the width of the skull expressed as a percentage of its length. For instance, if the skull length is 200 mm., and its width 160 mm., the cephalic index will be 80, and the head-form is termed mesocephalic.

[8] P. 33, German ed.

ARE THE JEWS A RACE?

Here again, we find the characteristics of the Jews coinciding with those of the nations among which they live. The Caucasians among whom they live are brachycephalic. In Arabia, Mesopotamia and Northern Africa, the Jews are as distinctly dolichocephalic as the races native to these regions. European Jews, like the rest of the Europeans, are midway between these extremes.

Within Europe itself the cephalic index of Jews and non-Jews shows striking coincidences within the same region. Thus, Fishberg found the average cephalic indexes in the following countries to be:

Country	Average Cephalic Index of Jews	of Non-Jews
Lithuania	81.05	81.88
Rumania	81.82	82.92
Hungary	82.45	81.40
Poland	81.91	82.13
Little Russia	82.45	82.31
Galicia	83.33	84.40 [9]

In general, we find a great uniformity of head forms among both Jews and non-Jews in Eastern Europe; there is but slight divergence; this condition is attributed by the American anthropologist, Ripley, to "the perfect monotony and uniformity of environment of the Russian people", to the unvarying conditions of nature "from the Carpathian Mountains, east and north".[10]

[9] Fishberg, p. 52.
[10] Fishberg, p. 51.

PHYSICAL CHARACTERISTICS

What becomes now of the so-called immutable, sharply-defined race type of the Jews which "may be traced with equal certainty through the course of thousands of years"? We cannot even find such sharply-defined traits in our own day.

Being unable to prove the existence of the Jewish race type by those traits which are generally regarded as racial indications, the advocates of the presence of a distinct Jewish race are obliged to turn from anthropological to physiological traits. The Jew is to be distinguished, they say, not by the appearance of his body, but by its posture.

We are already leaving the ground of comparatively unchanging factors and entering the field of very alterable factors. Among Jews the chest measurement is declared to be strikingly small, menstruation to appear very early in life, their fruitfulness is said to attain extremely high figures, their adaptability to climate to be extremely great. On the whole, these statements appear quite true, but do no seem to be "Jewish characteristics" at all, if we take the pains to compare the Jews not with the totality of the population among whom they live, but with the classes in which Jews are most commonly found. It will then be found that narrow chests are as common among non-Jews who are accustomed—because they are merchants or intellectuals—to a sedentary mode of life, with little physical exercise, and that menstruation, not only among Jewesses, but among all city women, appears earlier than among country girls.

ARE THE JEWS A RACE?

The faculty of acclimatisation in the tropics is possessed by the Jew in common with the other Europeans who visit those climates as merchants, not as soldiers or heavy labourers, and who are able to abstain from alcohol. For hard physical exertion and alcohol are the greatest enemy of the European in the tropics. We cannot consider the Jew's faculty of acclimatisation as a specific Jewish quality unless we assume that alcoholism is one of the immutable race traits of the dominant blond race.

As for their fruitfulness, which has resulted in making the Jews as numerous as the grains of sand on the seashore, this property also reveals how great is the dependence of "immutable race traits" on social conditions. As in all other urban populations, the Jewish population of cities also presents a distinct decline in the birth rate. This fact is well known in the case of Western Europe, but is even beginning to be observed in Eastern Europe. In Rumania, the rate of living births per thousand inhabitants shows the following changes:

	For the Population as a Whole	For the Jews Only
1871-1875	34.2%	46.5%
1881-1885	41.3%	46.8%
1901-1905	39.5%	32.6% [11]

The birth rate of the Jews was considerably higher than that of the entire population thirty years ago, but is now considerably lower.

[11] Fishberg, German ed., p. 229.

PHYSICAL CHARACTERISTICS

In Western Europe and America the fruitfulness of the Jews is decreasing as rapidly as the general fruitfulness of the population of France. In fact, if the present tendency continues, it will actually mean the dying out of the Jews, which would be the most original manner of solving the entire Jewish question.

In Prussia, the excess of births over deaths per thousand of respective population groups was:

| | Natural Increase | |
	Jews	Christians
1885	10.33	12.29
1890	7.64	12.58
1895	6.66	15.12
1900	4.52	14.57
1905	3.34	12.93
1908	3.33	14.97 [12]

"In certain German cities the birth and death rates of the Jews are almost equal; in Breslau in 1906-1907, there were registered 507 Jewish births and 694 Jewish deaths. Here they do not replenish the earth." [13]

Interesting figures are communicated by Felix Theilhaber in a book entitled *Sterile Berlin*,[14] which contains far more information than is suggested by the title, being in fact a thorough discussion of the entire modern population problem.

[12] Fishberg, p. 69.
[13] Fishberg, German ed., p. 60.
[14] *Das sterile Berlin*, Berlin, 1913.

ARE THE JEWS A RACE?

Theilhaber had already issued in 1911 a book bearing the ominous title: *The Destruction of the German Jews.*[15] In the work above mentioned he communicates a number of new calculations based on Berlin conditions, referring to the relative number of Jewish births in that city:

	Number of Jews, 15-45 Years of Age	Jewish Births	Births per 1,000 Jews of Child-bearing Age
1880	13,300	1,497	112
1895	22,678	1,694	75
1900	24,531	1,649	67
1905	25,491	1,630	64
1910 approx. ..	24,000	1,306	54

If the Jewish births are to replace the losses by death, there would have to be seventy-eight births per 1,000 Jewish women of child-bearing age. But with the present birth rate, 1,000 Jewish couples, in other words, "2,000 Jews of child-producing age, have a total offspring of only 1,400 persons, equivalent to a dying out of one-third their number. If this should continue to be the condition, the Jews of Berlin will, after two or three generations—in other words, in 80-120 years—be almost extinct." [16]

Of course, we are here ignoring immigration from other regions. At any rate, our figures are sufficient to show that the "infinite fruitfulness of the Jews" as an "immutable" race trait is a non-existent quantity.

[15] *Der Untergang der deutschen Juden.*
[16] *Das sterile Berlin,* pp. 106-107.

PHYSICAL CHARACTERISTICS

Physiology having transpired to be as poor a basis as anthropology, pathology is called upon for assistance. The race traits which a healthy Jew is incapable of contributing are now sought in the Jew suffering from disease. It is maintained that the Jew is more subject to certain diseases than the non-Jew, while he is less subject to others than the non-Jew. But here again we are dealing only with hasty generalisations.

Diabetes (sugar), for example, is commonly considered a "Jewish sickness". As a matter of fact, many Jews do die of this disease.

"From Auerbach's *Analysis of the Demography of the Jews in Budapest*, it appears that of the 487 deaths reported as due to diabetes in 1902-07, 238, or more than one-half, occurred in Jews, although they only constituted 22.6 per cent. of the population. The rates were 5.9 deaths due to diabetes per 100,000 Catholics and 21.4 per 100,000 Jews.[17]

But comparisons of this kind between Jews and non-Jews are quite misleading, whether they are concerned with diseases or with criminality or with school attendance. We know that certain diseases are more common in certain vocations and social strata than others. A comparison between Jews and non-Jews is legitimate when the non-Jews are compared with Jews of those classes to which most of the Jews belong. Proceeding in this manner, we shall observe that diabetes is a very common complaint among

[17] Fishberg, pp. 297-298.

merchants and intellectuals, including non-Jewish merchants and intellectuals. Accordingly, Fishberg determined that diabetes is a specifically Jewish disease only in places where the Jews are predominantly in business. In New York, German Jews, according to the records of the hospitals, suffer from diabetes three times as frequently as non-Jews. The Russian Jews, on the other hand, most of whom are workers, do not show a higher percentage of diabetes than that of the population as a whole. Diabetes also is, therefore, not a race disease but a class disease.

On the other hand, it is declared that Jews are not so susceptible to certain diseases as non-Jews; such diseases are: cholera, smallpox, tuberculosis, etc. Where this declaration agrees with the facts, it may be explained by the social conditions of the Jews, who, in Germany, for instance, are members of the wealthier classes, are less addicted to alcohol, and are always more inclined to consult a physician at once, while the uneducated masses of the people usually regard physicians with mistrust. Even the most orthodox, most superstitious Jew will not seek to oppose the epidemic by prayers and sacrifices alone, as is the custom among the Italian and Russian masses.

"As a matter of fact, it is well known to every physician of experience among the Jews that they are always ready to take advantage of every new measure to prevent or cure disease. There are practically no anti-vaccinationists among them; nor are there any other kind of cranks among them to urge them on to resist the attempts on the part of the authorities to vaccinate them. The Jewish clergy is always in favour of placing medical matters in the hands of physicians and is not in favour of leaving such matters in the hands of Providence." [18]

Shall we consider ignorance among the masses as a race trait of the "Aryans"? For the present, we still explain such traits by the social and political conditions in which the nations live.

It appears that disease as a race trait also is a poor argument. There remains for the advocates of Jewish racial purity a single refuge, the last refuge of the race theorists who aim to construct races on the basis of the modern nations, namely, *language*.

Of course, language as a race trait is particularly unreliable in the case of the Jews, more unreliable than in any other human group, since the Jews—with the exception of the Polish and Russian Jews—everywhere speak the language of their environment. Unable to use the criterion of language in the case of the Jews, the criterion of *pronunciation* is resorted to. We are told the Jew may always be recognised by his pronunciation. In all the languages he speaks, the Jew has his Jewish accent. Said the famous African explorer, Gerhart Rohlfs:

"We know that the Jew in Germany can always be recognised by his discordant accent. The same is the case with the Jews in all European countries . . . also in Northern Africa."

[18] Fishberg, p. 128.

And Andree says:

"The so-called Jewish accent (*mauscheln*) is a Jewish race trait, as ineradicable in them as the Jewish type itself. . . . This is very decidedly a race trait, since it is found among the Jews of all countries." [19]

Richard Wagner's reasoning to show that the Jew is incapable of producing good music is based on the so-called Jewish pronunciation. After pointing out in his essay, "The Jews in Music",[20] that the physical appearance of the Jew always has for us an "unpleasantly foreign quality: we involuntarily feel that we desire to have nothing to do with a person who has this appearance", he continues:

"Far more important—in fact, of decisive importance—is the nature of the influence of the Jew's pronunciation upon us; particularly, this is the essential point of departure in a study of the Jewish influence on music. . . . Particularly repulsive to us is the purely sensual manifestation of the Jewish language. Civilisation has not succeeded in surmounting the peculiar stubbornness of the Jewish character in the matter of the Semitic mode of pronunciation, in spite of their two thousand years of contact with European nations. Our ear feels the absolutely foreign and unpleasant sound of a certain hissing, strident, lisping and choking pronunciation in the Jewish speech; a distortion and peculiar rearrangement of the words and of phrase constructions, entirely foreign to our national lan-

[19] Fishberg, German ed., p. 77.
[20] *Das Judentum in der Musik.*

guage, finally imparts to this pronunciation the character of a confused babbling, to listen to which causes our attention to dwell rather on this repulsive *manner* of the Jewish speech, than on the substance it conveys. The exceptional importance of this circumstance in explaining the impression made upon us by the musical works of modern Jews must be recognised and emphasised from the outset. . . . If the quality of his mode of speech makes it almost impossible for a Jew to acquire the ability of an artistic expression of his feelings and views through *speech*, his capacity for manifesting such moods and thoughts in *song* must be even far inferior, etc."

No doubt a Siegfried speaking with a Jewish accent would be impossible on the stage. Richard Wagner's dialect was not a Jewish dialect but that of Saxony. If we should use Wagner's arguments, we might say:

"Civilisation has not succeeded in surmounting the peculiar stubbornness of the Saxon character in the matter of the Saxon mode of pronunciation, in spite of their two thousand years of contact with European nations." But it is not unreasonable to assume that Direktor Striese in *The Rape of the Sabine Women*[21] would hardly do much better in the rôle of Siegfried than the well-known Schmock.[22] Would

21 Direktor Striese, a character who speaks in the Saxon dialect in the farce, *Der Raub der Sabinerinnen* (1885), by Franz von Schönthan (1849-1913) and Paul von Schönthan (1853-1905).

22 Schmock is a Jewish journalist in Freytag's (1816-1895) play *Die Journalisten*, who speaks German with exaggerated Jewish mannerisms.

it be reasonable to assume that the influence of the Saxons on music could not but be disastrous?

Pronunciation is a most peculiar element in language. Grammar and vocabulary may be fixed in writing and taught through books; pronunciation may be but roughly indicated by our limited alphabet; it cannot be precisely set down. To learn to pronounce, we must be in personal contact with persons who speak the language as natives. Pronunciation is far more tenacious in its retention of the influences of the life of the people, of the masses, than are grammar and vocabulary, which may be fixed in writing and thus isolated from life. The differences between the dialects are chiefly differences of pronunciation. Furthermore, contrary to the condition in the case of grammar and vocabulary, which may be learned by purely theoretical means, the acquisition of a correct pronunciation requires constant practice of tongue and ear.

If a child has practised no other pronunciation than that of his home dialect, it will be difficult for him to get rid of this dialectic tinge. Very few persons have so fine a hearing and so ready a tongue as to be able to acquire the correct pronunciation of a foreign language late in life, or, for that matter, of a strange dialect. Even those persons who are complete masters of the foreign language, who speak it fluently, will reveal in their pronunciation that they are not speaking their mother-tongue. On the other hand, having less occasion to practise their own language when abroad, these persons will forget its words

and its constructions more easily than its pronunciation. I
met German workers living in England who had been in
that country since their childhood, and who were already
having difficulty in speaking German at all—in fact, who
preferred to speak English—but whose pronunciation both
of German and English revealed the part of Germany
from which they had come.

If the Jews have their specific accent always and everywhere—so do the Saxons, so do the Swabians. Does this
justify us in erecting race traits on this basis? In Saxony
everybody speaks with a Saxon accent, regardless of his
country of origin. On the other hand, the children of
Saxon parents, if they are raised in Württemberg, will not
speak the Saxon dialect but the Swabian dialect; they will
speak Bavarian in München and Plattdeutsch on the Baltic
coast. Pronunciation is no more hereditary than vocabulary and grammar, but acquired. It is acquired, however,
in a somewhat different manner, and the environment of the
individual is a more important factor.

If the Jews have a different pronunciation of the languages of the nations among whom they live than these
nations themselves, this proves only that the Jews form a
separate community in the individual nations, thus remaining in close contact with each other; only to the extent that
they lead such a separate existence will they preserve their
peculiar pronunciation. Jews that have not been raised
in a closed Jewish community but together with non-Jewish
people will have as little of the Jewish accent as the other

people. There is a well-known anecdote of a Jewish boy sent by his father into the country in order that he might get rid of the Jewish accent. When his father calls for him at the expiration of a year, he finds to his horror that little Baruch has not only not relinquished his Jewish pronunciation but has imparted it to the entire village.

Little Baruch's infectious influence deserves all our respect, but an anecdote of this type could be considered as having scientific value only by a Sombart or by the protagonists of Jewish ritual murder. The so-called Jewish accent disappears more quickly even than their narrowness of chest when they begin to live in a different social environment. The fact that some persons have sought to elevate this condition into a race trait proves only that there are persons who would represent the Jews as a separate race at any cost, and who yet are put in the most embarrassing position if asked to state what are the permanent and unmistakable traits of this race.

The Jews of the present day are not a pure race, either geographically or chronologically; even the most superficial acquaintance with their history will prove this statement. Judaism arose on the soil of Palestine, a border region between two areas, each of which embraces a distinct race, probably the result of the peculiarities of the two regions: in Palestine, the foot-hills of mountainous Asia Minor (in the widest sense of the word, therefore, including Armenia), whence originated the Armenoid type, and the beginnings of the extensive steppes of Arabia, extending as far as Mesopotamia. In the latter regions there arose the type commonly designated as the Semitic type, but which might perhaps better be ascribed to a certain area and not to a certain language group, namely, the Arabian type. Some members of the Armenoid type must be counted with the Semitic language family; for example, the Assyrians.[23]

Both these geographical races must have come in contact, at an early period, as well as repeatedly thereafter, and have intermingled at their border points, therefore in Palestine also. Primitive Israelitic history is of course still very obscure: the reports in the Bible are absolutely unreliable. But there is no doubt among scholars that the population of Palestine must have constituted a mixture of races at a very early period, however greatly they may differ in minor points.

But Palestine was a border region in another sense also. The "spheres of influence"—to use a modern term—of the first two great states of the historical era, of Babylonia and Egypt, met in Palestine. Before the development of navigation on the Mediterranean, the entire commercial intercourse between these two empires passed through Palestine, which also afforded passage for their military forces, and often even served as their battleground.

Palestine has, therefore, seen merchants with their slaves and mercenaries, who often came from great distances, and belonged to the most varied races. The mercenaries often

[23] Cf. among others, Eduard Meyer, *Geschichte des Altertums*, 2nd ed., i, ii, p. 377 *et seq.*

remained garrisoned in the fortresses of Palestine for long periods. Such elements have never failed to provide a numerous posterity in any country in which they have been stationed.

Furthermore, the Israelites were at first by no means averse to conjugal relations with persons of other races. Stade informs us on this point:

"The people of Israel were no more a people of pure blood than any other people on earth: for, in addition to Canaanitic, Hebraic, Arabic components, individuals of Aramaic and Egyptian origin were also absorbed by them.

"How slight was the effort they made to be exclusive is apparent from the circumstance that we meet with an Ishmaelite in David's family. In addition, the ancient Israelites were distinctly surprised by the timidity with which the ancient Egyptians guarded themselves against any contact with foreigners.[24] Of course, this does not mean that the Jews did not prize their own nationality and the purity of their Israelitic origin. But since such purity was surely quite unusual in the oldest period, its absence was not considered a blemish. This makes it easy for us to understand that while, according to the most ancient form of the legend, Isaac, the son of promise, was to have married a woman of his kindred, it is narrated without

[24] Compare Genesis xliii, 32, where we read of Joseph and his brothers: "And they set on for him by himself, and for them by themselves, and for the Egyptians, which did eat with him by themselves: because the Egyptians might not eat bread with the Hebrews; for that is an abomination unto the Egyptians."

110

apparent surprise that other fathers marry foreign women: Judah, a Canaanitic woman; Joseph, an Egyptian woman." [25]

While the position of Palestine facilitated the incursion of foreign elements and an intermingling with them, it also facilitated the spreading of the inhabitants of the country among their neighbours. Being a poor, unproductive country, Palestine was likely to suffer from excess of population. It was too small and weak, the superior power of its neighbours too crushing, to enable Palestine to dispose of its population by settling it in conquered regions. The territory of the Phœnicians cut Palestine off from good seaports and the practice of navigation. Therefore the path of colonisation beyond the seas was also closed to the Israelites. Their surplus population had no other alternative than to go abroad as merchants (sometimes as mercenaries, but these played no important part in history). In this capacity, they travelled further and further and founded a number of settlements. In many cities they became so numerous as to conduct not only trading operations, but also to employ artisans of their own; the number of their intellectuals also increased.

Constantly crowded and congested in their homeland by the overwhelming strength of their neighbours, this little race had no other path of expansion. This path was pursued so energetically that the Israelitic population abroad finally became more numerous than the home population.

[25] Stade, *Geschichte des Volkes Israel,* vol. i, p. 111.

ARE THE JEWS A RACE?

The home population repeatedly loses its status as an independent nation, finally losing it forever. But before this time had come, the centre of gravity of Judaism had been shifted from its original location to a number of cities in Egypt, Syria and Mesopotamia.

As long as the Israelites had remained in Palestine, the uniform natural environment necessarily favored the existence of a tendency in the direction of the production of a uniform geographical race, thereby somewhat opposing the differentiation of types resulting from race mixture. But their migrations and their distribution to the most different natural environments completely abolished this tendency toward a uniform geographical race. But the mixture of races, which was already traditional, now went on with redoubled speed.

The greater number of the Jews now lived outside of their homeland. Strangers among strangers, tolerated only, quite often regarded with hostility, they found no support in the little nation whose capital was Jerusalem. They could maintain themselves only by observing the most intimate unity among them. This unity applied not only to the specific locality, but also to all the localities; there was a sort of interlocal solidarity. In the immense region over which they were spread, they were never simultaneously persecuted, plundered, exiled, in all their colonies. If such events came to pass in one region, the victims, the despoiled and homeless, always found active assistance and support in other regions.

112

PHYSICAL CHARACTERISTICS

But this unified organisation became less and less national. The Jews had never constituted a uniform race; they now ceased to be even a nation. Everything that constitutes the essence of a nation had been lost to them; they had lost their common land, even their common language.

"The Jews living abroad had to speak the foreign tongue, and if several generations had already been living abroad, the younger generations finally would be able to speak only the language of their native country, forgetting their mother tongue. Greek particularly became very popular among them. Already in the Third Century B.c., the sacred writings of the Jews were translated into Greek, probably for the reason that but few Alexandrian Jews still understood Hebrew and possibly also for purposes of propaganda among the Greeks. . . . Several centuries before the destruction of Jerusalem by the Romans, Hebrew already ceased to be a living tongue." [26]

There remained to the Jews of their existence as a nation practically only their national aspiration, their desire to become a nation again, and as no bounds may be set to man's wishes, they felt that this nation would be headed by an indomitable saviour, the Messiah. But, as a matter of actual fact, the Jews were becoming more and more transformed from a nation into an international association. Their bond of union was the remnant of their ancient

[26] Karl Kautsky, *Foundations of Christianity*, New York, 1925, pp. 257, 258.

national life that was still maintained, namely, their religion. But precisely the religions, in the form of myth and philosophy, were in a state of constant flux in the centuries before and after the birth of Christ, particularly in the circles from which the Jews were then exclusively recruited, namely, the populations of the cities. The firm and tangible symbol of the Jews' community was not the *philosophy* of religion, but the religious *ceremonial;* this it was that served the Jews of all the regions then involved in world traffic as the bond recognised and recognisable by all. And simultaneously as a means of keeping outsiders out.

We must not infer that the Jews aimed to preserve a rigid exclusiveness toward all new elements. On the contrary, with the progress of their loss of a national existence, and their assumption of the character of a mere international association for mutual aid, we find a simultaneous increase of the desire to swell their ranks by means of propaganda and thus to acquire new forces. Conquests of new territory were impossible under the circumstances; propaganda was resorted to.

" 'But woe unto you, scribes and Pharisees, hypocrites!' the gospel lays these words into the mouth of Jesus, 'for ye compass sea and land to make one proselyte and, when he is made, ye make him twofold more a child of hell than yourselves'." [27]

I have treated the causes and effects of this propaganda

[27] Matthew xxiii, 15; Kautsky, *ibid.,* p. 260.

in full detail in my *Foundations of Christianity*.[28] It would
lead us too far afield to go over all this ground again. It is
sufficient to state here that this propaganda met with
great success; and the greater the success, the more necessary would it, of course, seem to be to keep aloof from all
undependable newcomers. The strict observation of the
ritual prescriptions now became doubly necessary. In
Freemasonry we find a similar rich development of ceremonial which, particularly for intelligent persons, frequently makes a very stupid impression, and is valuable
only because it serves as a means of making it difficult for
frivolous interlopers to gain admission. Those who subjected themselves permanently to the Jewish rite might
be depended upon as reliable fellow-members.

But every stranger was welcome who would recognise
this rite—without regard to origin. Jewish exclusiveness
was not an exclusiveness of race. The Jewish propaganda
in all the regions of the ancient world was rather calculated
to stimulate tremendously the mingling of races within
Judaism.

In spite of the great success of this propaganda, it did
not take hold of the masses of the pagan peoples. These
rather displayed an increasing aversion to Judaism, as the
latter ceased to constitute a nation and became an international league. The more Judaism lost the character of
a nation, the more did it cease to embrace all the classes
of society as then known, now including only the urban

28 Kautsky, *ibid.*, pp. 253-264

groups, in many cases only those concerned with commercial and financial business. As long as the Jews had been a nation, and a very small nation at that, they had been a source of concern to their nearest neighbours—by reason of their aspirations for expansion or for maintaining themselves—only in occasional instances. The more they developed into a league of members of a specific class, spread throughout the world, the more were they involved in the class struggles of the entire world. And this in a two-fold manner. In the first place, they were drawn into the struggles of their own class against other classes, and in the second place, they were also drawn into conflicts with competitors within their own class, for this class was much annoyed by the strength drawn by the Jews from their international dissemination and solidarity. These two varieties of class struggle were ultimately combined in a manner that was quite uncomfortable for the Jews: competitors in their own commercial class made efforts to turn aside the hostility of other classes, particularly to the Jewish members of their class, thus transforming struggles against middlemen, tax farmers, usurers, into struggles against the Jews. This distortion of conditions was favoured by the fact that the Jews were defenceless foreigners, and also—to just as great a degree—by those properties of the Jews by which they sought to maintain themselves, since they *were* defenceless foreigners, by their close union and their international solidarity. Elements of the population thus constituted easily become suspicious in the eyes

116

of popular masses with local prejudices. It was just as easy in the Seventeenth and Eighteenth Centuries, in England, to instigate a massacre of Catholics for the most trivial causes as it was throughout the last two thousand years to inaugurate occasional pogroms against the Jews everywhere in Europe. But no one has ever thought of ever designating the English persecutions of Catholics as race struggles and the English Catholics as a peculiar, "pure race".

The situation became a desperate one for the Jews when the Government authorities also rose against them. Before Cæsarism felt itself firm in the saddle, it had considered the Jews to be a valuable ally. But as imperial absolutism became solidified, it became more suspicious of all independent organisations, including Judaism. And when the Jews of Jerusalem went so far as to seek to maintain their independence as opposed to the Romans, by actual warfare, Judaism was completely outlawed.[29]

From now on, the propaganda of Judaism was deprived of every foundation; everywhere the Jews were forced into the defensive, all accessions from non-Jewish circles were cut off. The Jews then became a caste which had to increase by inbreeding, within their own ranks. For the first time, the isolation of the Jews became quite marked.

This condition found its culmination in the ghetto of the feudal era, in the Jewish quarters in which the Jewish population of each city was strictly confined. This condi-

[29] Kautsky, *ibid.*, pp. 167-171.

tion might perhaps have succeeded in maintaining the Jews as a pure race if they had been a pure race to begin with. But the Jews never were a pure race, and even at the period of their most stringent isolation there were two conditions opposing the formation of a uniform race.

The Jews could not become a geographical race, for their settlements extended over the most varied and distant countries. On the other hand, even if the Jews had originally constituted a pure race, they could not have maintained their purity, owing to the impossibility of preventing a mingling with foreign elements.

Precisely the period of the most rigid isolation of the Jews is also the period of their greatest legal disability, subjecting them to one persecution after another. They were not robbed only of their valuables; not only were men slain, but women were violated in great numbers. But the posterity of these women were considered as Jews and bred as such. Even though we should assume that all Jewish women had always been inaccessible to the seductive arts of their non-Jewish neighbours, the fact of the persecutions of the Jews alone would be sufficient to preclude the possibility of an immutable "purity" of Jewish blood during the last two thousand years. A mixed race from the very outset, the Jews, in the course of their migrations, have come into contact with a great succession of new races, and their blood has thus become more and more mixed.

We have already pointed out the significant fact that the

PHYSICAL CHARACTERISTICS

Jews of each region present many physical traits in common with the non-Jewish population of the same region. This may, perhaps, be an effect of like natural conditions on both Jews and non-Jews. But it is just as plausible to assume that it may be the result of a sexual contact between Jews and non-Jews. Probably the case is the same as in the world of organisms in general: both factors, adaptation and heredity, have had considerable to do with the determination of bodily traits.

But the non-Jews among whom the Jews live are no less a mixed race than the Jews themselves. Jewish blood flows in their veins also. It is not only the extra-conjugal relations between—let us say—Jewish business men or students and Christian servant girls or waitresses that makes many a Christian child an "offspring of the Jews". Perhaps even more Jewish blood was transmitted to the body of the Christian population by the conversion of Jews, a process which has been going on for centuries. In Spain, for example, in the Fourteenth and Fifteenth Centuries, hundreds of thousands of Jews were converted to Christianity. Their posterity infected the Aryan race with their blood. There is no Jew today who can say to himself with certainty that he has not a drop of non-Jewish blood in his veins, if only for the reason that there never has existed a Jewish race either in the sense of a pure breed of domestic animals or in the other sense, that of a geographical race.

But even if we should assume that all those who were

119

following the ritual laws of the Jews two thousand years ago constituted a specific race, no Jew of the present day can assert with absolute sureness that his ancestors included only elements that had descended from the Jews of that period.

On the other hand, also, there is not a single Christian who can declare with absolute certainty that his own antecedents include no Jew among their members.

No race traits can be mentioned which could be used as a criterion for determining this question. The "Jewish countenance", black hair, flashing eyes, and particularly the aquiline nose, heritages from one of the many races out of which the Jews were built up, cannot serve as a criterion, no matter how outspoken these traits may be considered to be, for they are found also, as we have seen, among many non-Jewish races. Furthermore, they are found only among a small fraction of the Jews themselves. This characteristic countenance has probably become associated with the Jewish type, as in those regions of Northern Europe in which the Jews lived together in rather great numbers, namely, east of the Elbe and north of the Carpathians, it is less frequent among the non-Jews, and therefore most sharply distinguished from the countenance found in the most frequent types, and therefore most striking.

Yet even in those regions, the "Jewish face" does not of itself determine the Jewish type. Particularly striking qualities of dress and *coiffure*, kaftan and *pajes* (side curls), pronunciation, bodily carriage, play of the features, and gesticulations—all of which are social peculiarities, handed down by more or less involuntary imitation of one's environment—must cooperate with the hereditary Jewish face in order to make the unmistakable, the "correct" Jewish type apparent.

The cartoonists of the comic papers are quite justified in depicting Jews as possessing the "Jewish countenance". The task of the caricaturist is to exaggerate and emphasize striking and unusual traits. But when anthropologists dignify this countenance by making it an earmark of a specific Jewish race, they are creating a caricature of their own science. Werner Sombart, of course, imagines that Jews may always be detected by their faces:

"A later age will hardly find it possible to believe that persons existed in our day who were incapable of distinguishing the Jew as a member of a specific nation or of a specific race (it does not at all matter whether the Jews be called Jews or not) from a Negro or an Eskimo, or a Pomeranian, or a Southern Frenchman", and this is the more culpable, for: "Our eye has been obviously much sharpened, owing to training in the natural sciences, in its ability to detect the influence of the blood in man, during the last generation." [30]

This sharp eye has been rendered so acute in the case of Sombart that it is sufficient for him to cast a glance at a portrait, even though it be but a wood-cut or a copper

[30] Werner Sombart, *Die Zukunft der Juden*, pp. 50, 55.

engraving, to determine at once whether the original was a Jew or not:

"It is well known that the Governor-General of the Dutch East Indian Company who, though he may not be considered as the founder of the Dutch power in Java, nevertheless contributed much to the solidification of this power, bore the name of Cohn (Coen). And we can easily convince ourselves that he was not the only Jewish governor of the Dutch East Indian possessions, if we glance through a set of portraits of these officials." [31]

If a man's name is Coen, Sombart, owing to his acute sense of the blood in man, "knows" that his name was Cohn, and that he was a Jew. Those who are acquainted with the Dutch colonial policy, and who "know" more of Coen than his name, are of course aware that Coen had nothing to do with Cohn, and that he was as little a Jew as the other governors whose portraits have been examined by our conscientious professor. [32]

By means of the same profound method, Sombart declares the Scotchman Law as likely to have been a Jew, for Law might have been Levy and in "*many* (!) of his pictures" he looks Jewish!

Another example of this splendid method is the following, also taken from Sombart: "In order to prove the significance of the *Jews* as financiers in France, it is sufficient

[31] Werner Sombart, *Die Juden und das Wirtschaftsleben*, pp. 30, 31.
[32] Cf. W. v. Ravesteijn, *Kapitalismus und Judentum, Die Neue Zeit*, vol. xxx, part 2, pp. 714, 715.

to recall the influential position occupied by Samuel Bernard during the later portion of the reign of Louis XIV and the entire reign of Louis XV." [33]

In other words, to prove the importance of the *Jews*, "it is sufficient" for Sombart to remind us of a *single* Jew. This is quite funny, and is made even funnier if this Jew should happen to be not a Jew. Sombart's critic in the *Archiv für Sozialwissenschaft und Sozialpolitik*, Julius Guttmann, has the following to say on this subject.

"In so important a country as France, the Jews remained for a long time of very subordinate importance as financiers. The only great Jewish financier discovered by Sombart as far down as the Eighteenth Century is Samuel Bernard. Bernard, according to the evidence of his baptismal certificate, which has been long available, was a Christian by birth, and the only circumstance that could be adduced in favour of his Jewish descent would be the fact that his father and grandfather had already lived in France as painters." [34]

Houston Stewart Chamberlain seems to be just as skilful in detecting the "influence of the blood", for he declares concerning Marx and Engels that they were two "highly gifted Jews, who sought to transplant to Europe from Asia many of the best thoughts of their race". [35]

---

[33] Sombart. *Die Juden und das Wirtschaftsleben*, p. 56.
[34] *Archiv für Sozialwissenschaft und Sozialpolitik*, vol. xxxvi, p. 159.
[35] *Die Grundlagen des neunzehnten Jahrhunderts*, 1899, vol. ii, p. 835.

ARE THE JEWS A RACE?

The "scientific" method of the Sombart and Chamberlain school of Jewish studies was already anticipated by our friend Schönlank more than twenty years ago in a delightful parody in the *feuilleton* of the *Vorwärts*—it happened to be an April First number—in which he proved that Hammerstein, the well-known editor-in-chief of the *Kreuzzeitung*, was of Jewish extraction, originally bearing the name Chamer Stein. And how about Chamer Laihn— has not this name also a Jewish sound, Mr. Chamberlain?

CHAPTER VI

MENTAL QUALITIES OF THE JEWISH RACE

THERE is not much to be gotten, therefore, out of the bodily traits of the Jewish race. Even the racial anti-Semites themselves do not display any very great confidence in the certainty of such traits, in spite of all their bombast concerning the profound natural gulf separating the Jewish race from the other races. They are very careful not to draw practical inferences from their race theories, or to demand—let us say—the political disfranchisement, the prohibition against marrying "Aryan" persons, or the elimination from Europe of every man who displays a "Jewish countenance". Nor do they recognise every man as an Aryan who fails to possess this countenance. They are finally brought to the pass of recognising as the natural "race trait" of the Jews only the records of the Bureau of Vital Statistics.

But of course, the wickedness and disaster involved in the Jewish race is not based upon the peculiarity of their *bodily* traits, but on their *mental* traits, not on their hooked noses and crooked legs, but on their crooked morality. The high intelligence, the close solidarity of the Jews, are not virtues but vices. For they make the evil qualities of the Jews more dangerous, namely, his importunity, his destructive, purely negative criticism, and, particularly, his heartless, ruthless desire for gain. In order to prove that the Jew is a born criminal, our racial anti-Semites bring no more destructive argument to bear than the overwhelming assertion that the Jew is a born capitalist. They claim that all the vulgarity of the capitalist mode of thought, which the Teutonic individual has had the greatest difficulty in acquiring, has been inherent in the Jewish blood from the beginning of history. Long before the slightest trace of capitalism was in existence, the Jew had already been impregnated by some miracle with the capitalist mode of thought and feeling, an undistinguishable race trait for all times and countries, and in all modes of production. It is therefore not surprising that the Jew leaves all his competitors far behind in the game of capitalist competition, thus injuring the Christian proletarians beyond repair by causing them to be exploited not only by "blond beasts" who had to be artificially trained to this capitalist viciousness.

The thorn in the flesh of these theorists is the mental qualities of the Jews. The fact that these qualities include a number that were unpleasant to their Jewish neighbours was an observation frequently made long before the days of the racial anti-Semites. But formerly these traits had been ascribed to their peculiar social situation, to their oppression, their limitation to a few fixed callings. It had formerly been assumed that with the elimination of this exceptional situation, these peculiarities also would dis-

126

appear. Under these circumstances, a criticism of the Jews usually developed into a criticism of state and society and into a demand for social and political reforms. But it is possible to escape the necessity of making such demands if the mental qualities of the Jews are considered to be an inextinguishable race trait.

"Race alone may often serve only to cloak our ignorance," says Fishberg, "particularly if all the conditions of the environment have been ignored." [1]

No doubt this is often the case. But just as frequently we find "race" resorted to as a means of preventing any criticism of society, any effort to secure its further evolution, or even the investigation of its nature, the conception of race being used in such instances in order to nullify the influence of the milieu—including also the artificial, social milieu—on man.

We have observed in the preceding chapter that the Jews are a mixed race, but we were nevertheless in a position to indicate the traces of the bodily traits of one of the geographical races of which this mixture is composed. We can no longer say anything concerning its mental traits, for mental traits are so intangible and variable that it is difficult if not impossible to assign *permanent* mental traits with definiteness to a certain race. This impossibility becomes the greater in the case of a prehistoric race of which no written documents are preserved. We completely lack any material for determin-

[1] Fishberg, German ed., p. 86.

ing the mental qualities of the races out of which the population of Palestine was built up several thousands of years ago.

But it is very difficult even to outline the characteristics of a nation on the basis of its written evidence. It is even very daring to judge a man on the basis of certain of his writings. Many individualities express themselves differently in their writings than in their real character. Personal observation itself is not sufficient to enable us to grasp the entire inner life of an individual; in fact, the individual is in the dark concerning much of his own individuality. He is aware of his inner life only where it enters his consciousness, and even his conscious mental life is coloured, simplified, idealised, by memory.

What little information we have concerning the life of earlier races is in the form of certain expressions by certain individuals. It is as a rule entirely impossible to determine at this late date to what extent these expressions are typical, if only for the class involved, not to mention the entire people.

Such evidences are extremely important as a means of determining the course of events, the problems faced by the human beings of the period and people in question, the stage of their knowledge and ability, the goals of their aspirations, the natural and artificial environment in which they moved. But he who would go beyond these things, he who would infer their entire inner life from these materials, will be able as a rule to deliver merely the production of his own imagination; this product will be interesting chiefly as a characterisation of the investigator rather than of those investigated. Nothing is more difficult than to place oneself inside another's skin.

Even if there existed anywhere a civilised nation corresponding to a pure race, and which had preserved its race purity for thousands of years, we should not be able to trace its mental idiosyncrasies through these thousands of years with such precision as to be able to state which elements must be assigned to heredity and which to the influence of the environment.

But in the case of a mixed race, the mere attempt to make such a distinction would be ridiculous.

There is more likelihood of success if we begin, not with the race, not with the environment, not with the past, but with the present. In this case, we can at least determine to a certain extent, by means of numerous observations, what alterations in the mental character are produced at this day by alterations in the environment. Proceeding from this knowledge, we may then with a certain definiteness interpret many evidences of former times. For we are then proceeding from the known to an explanation of the unknown, while to make the assumption that any mental characteristic known to us is a race trait is equivalent to the opposite process of explaining the known by means of the unknown.

The former method, that which begins with the environment, is quite sufficient to explain the mental traits observable in the greater number of the Jews of the present day. We need only to note the influence of the urban environment on human beings at this day, the alterations in the country-dweller when exposed to the influence of city life, and then to recall that the Jews are the only race on earth that has constituted a purely urban population for approximately two thousand years: we now have an almost perfect explanation of Jewish traits. *They are an exaggerated form of urban traits in general.* I used the urban traits as early as 1890 in order to explain the Jewish character.[2] The Jew has become the city dweller *par excellence.* The uniformity of the artificial environment imparted to the Jews everywhere a uniform mental type, in spite of all the variations in their natural environment, and all the differences in the inherited race elements. If this uniform type should be accepted as a race type, the descendant of the *homo alpinus* might be designated as the *homo urbanus.*

Until long after the beginning of the Nineteenth Century, the circumstances under which the great masses of the population lived in cities were—regardless of the country or race concerned—so destructive that it was impossible for them to maintain their numbers by natural increase alone. If there had not been a constant accession of new forces from the country, they would have died out re-

[2] *Die Neue Zeit,* vol. viii, pp. 22 et seq. Cf. also my article, "Das Massaker von Kischeneff und die Judenfrage", *Die Neue Zeit,* vol. xxi, part 2, p. 303.

peatedly. A large fraction of the urban population consists everywhere of elements derived from the provinces; only an insignificant fraction can point to city ancestors for more than a century past. The Jews, however, have accomplished the astounding feat of so adapting themselves to urban life as not only to maintain themselves for two thousand years as an almost exclusively urban population, but even to increase in numbers under these conditions.

This may have been in part the operation of an unconscious process of selection, resulting in the elimination of all those unsuited to urban life. In the case of the non-Jewish population, this process was not necessary, since it was constantly interrupted by the accession of new elements from the country districts, who married into the established families, thus bringing about a mingling of selected and non-selected elements.

It is very questionable whether natural selection, in the form of the survival of the *fittest*, has had much influence on evolution. But there is no doubt that it has had an immense influence on the shaping and maintaining of species by means of the elimination of those *unfit* for the given environment.

In addition to this unconscious adaption, there is also a conscious adaptation. We have already pointed out that the Jew is far more inclined to consult a physician, and to observe the physician's orders conscientiously, than is the non-Jew, and also, that the Jew—at least in the ghetto—is far less addicted to alcohol. This difference between Jew and non-Jew is at bottom again merely a difference between city-dweller and country-dweller.

Owing to the conditions of his life, the latter is far superior to the city-dweller in strength; he is rarely ill. In the fullness of his strength, he despises disease. Owing to his love of displaying his vigour, and to his fear of appearing to be a weakling, he considers it a disgrace to be sick; besides, he is often too ignorant to have confidence in a physician.

The case with alcohol is similar. Alcohol is far less injurious to the vigorous peasant than to the neurasthenic city-dweller. And, the better his nervous state, the greater his muscular energy, the greater will be the quantities of alcohol he can consume without injury. Competitive drinking becomes a means of displaying bodily vigour, and he who avoids such tests is considered a coward.

There are no celebrations in the country without extensive intoxication. This condition occasionally leads to brawls, to murder and other killings, but otherwise has no injurious effect on the healthy peasant. In the city, where there is less opportunity for varied physical movement in the open air, and where the work to be accomplished is either more mental or more monotonous, and is performed in confined quarters and shops, the need of neutralising the feeling of an exhausted nervous condition becomes greater, the desire for alcohol is greater than in the country; the opportunities for obtaining alcohol are more numerous, but its effect is more destructive. This is clearly

132

apparent today, with great masses of the population living and working in cities, and with the present comparative, if not absolute cessation in the arrival of new elements from the country, as compared with the size of the city population. This condition, as well as the progress of a knowledge of physiology, is giving rise to a more and more energetic struggle with alcoholism. In this matter, the Jews have a lead of centuries, not in the requirement of abstinence, but in their abhorrence of intoxication; not so much because of a scientific knowledge, as because of their social position. The nations of the south are less inclined to be immoderate than those of the north. The Jews, coming from the south, and now living among Teutons and Slavs, being cut off from their environment, were not exposed to the temptations of this environment. Furthermore, the defenceless Jew was always far more exposed to danger than the non-Jew, and therefore sobriety was far more necessary to him. An intoxicated Jew who would transgress the laws would have brought great misfortune not only upon himself but upon the entire Jewry of his home town. This is perhaps the best explanation that can be offered for the moderation of the Jews. Although originally serving only to render the position of the Jews more secure, and perhaps practised as a habit handed down from their Oriental home, this abstinence has necessarily had an extremely favourable hygienic influence.

Of similar importance is the Jew's respect for learning, particularly for medicine. In the crude and ignorant condition which settled down over Europe during the migration of nations, the Jews were for a long time one of the few asylums still retaining remnants of ancient civilisation. As a result, they preserved a higher respect for science than their environment, and also practised science more intensively, except where this tendency was frustrated by the exclusiveness of the ghetto. The high level to which the art of healing had been developed among the Greeks was maintained in the first place by Jewish physicians, then further developed in the Orient, and passed on to the Arabs. Their better medical understanding was handed on to the Jews of the north from the Orient and from Spain.

By reason of a gradual natural selection, as well as owing to a conscious adaptation to their conditions of life, the Jews were finally enabled to resist the destructive influences of the city environment more successfully than the new arrivals from the provinces. While the non-Jewish city population was subject to constant renewal every few generations, the Jews had become a purely urban population.

The peculiarities of their historical position not only limited the Jews to the cities, but to certain callings within the cities.

They had to live as strangers among strangers, which is not so difficult for merchants. At first, merchants not only undertake to purchase and sell goods, but also to transport them, and such convoys of goods had often to

MENTAL QUALITIES

be personally conducted or at least personally supervised. The trade in commodities required that the merchants travel and sojourn in foreign countries, and all those nations which had a trade in commodities had adapted and accustomed themselves to the presence of foreign merchants among them.

The Jews, who found themselves compelled to leave their homeland, found it easiest to get along in foreign countries as merchants. Furthermore, it was those Jews whose mental makeup was best adapted to trade who were most likely to venture abroad.

In their original home the Jews, like any other nation, gave birth to all the classes and vocations natural to their social conditions. They displayed as little as any other people the mental limitation considered by anthropo-sociologists as the determining characteristic of the various races, namely, a turning of their faculties to one calling or to a few callings at most. They showed as much aptitude for agriculture as for trade and industry; as much for military service as for the art of government; as much for philosophy as for poetry. For the mind of the individual human being is far richer in its aptitudes than many a race theoretician can imagine. It is only the barriers of a narrow, monotonous life that cause an individual to develop only a few of his faculties to their full capacity, and perhaps to hand them on to his progeny in a more pronounced form, while other faculties may become stunted through desuetude.

The Jews outside of Palestine were therefore obliged to turn to trade chiefly. We therefore find them a trading nation at an early date. They thus must surely have developed emphatically those abilities needed by the merchant, and this great capacity must in the course of many generations of such activity within the same families have finally produced hereditary aptitudes and traits.

However, the Jews did not limit themselves to trade. Wherever possible, they resorted to other vocations also, particularly in cities where there were great numbers of Jews. Trade can never support more than a small minority, for trade is non-productive. Trade may under certain circumstances facilitate production but can never replace it. The Jews could not constitute a large fraction of the population of a city except where they were permitted to practise some other calling besides that of trade, perhaps a handicraft. On the other hand, where great numbers of Jews were living together, artisans and members of the liberal professions, such as physicians, who were of Jewish extraction, had better opportunities to maintain themselves as they found among their numerous co-religionists a strong support and an adequate market for their products and services. In antiquity, wherever the Jews lived together in great numbers, for instance, in Alexandria, we find also many artisans among them, in spite of that mysterious race predilection which is supposed to have made the commercial spirit an ineradicable characteristic of every Jew from the very beginning of history, in other words, long before there was any such thing as trade.

Being exclusively city-dwellers, they naturally did not favour those callings for which the new arrival from the country is best adapted, but those for which city life is the best preparation: such callings are those, on the one hand, which require much intelligence and theoretical knowledge, and which, on the other hand, do not demand much physical strength. When they turn to handicraft, they become, therefore, tailors rather than smiths, while the surplus of the merchant families, which cannot be absorbed in commerce, or which does not need to practise commerce, turns to purely mental labour.

Trade not only develops an excellent material foundation for mental labour, by favouring the prosperity of the families concerned, but far more by reason of the excellent natural talents encouraged by it. In my book, *Foundations of Christianity*, I already pointed out the connection between "trade and philosophy".[3] I have shown in that work that industry develops rather the abilities required by the reproductive arts, while trade develops rather the capacities for mathematical, abstract thought, but also for investigation and mental speculation, the tendency to associate with elements known those unknown elements that are necessarily connected with them. Furthermore, world commerce expands the horizon beyond that which is customary and traditional.

[3] *Op cit.*, pp. 203-208.

To be sure, scientific speculation is not to be regarded as identical with commercial speculation. But they differ not in the abilities required for them, but in the conditions of their application. Occupation with trade, investigation and speculation from an interested standpoint, are a great obstacle to disinterested investigation and speculation, in other words, to scientific work, and *vice versa*.

"Trade develops the necessary *ability* for scientific purposes, but not its *application* to scientific ends. On the contrary, where trade secures an influence over learning, its effect is entirely in the direction of doctoring the results of learning for its own purposes, of which our present-day bourgeois learning presents numerous examples.

"Scientific thought could only be developed in a class that was endowed with all the gifts, experience and knowledge involved in trade, but also liberated from the necessity of earning a living, and therefore possessing the necessary leisure, opportunity, and pleasure in disinterested investigation, in the solution of problems without regard to their immediate, practical and personal outcome." [4]

These conditions were realised in antiquity in some of the Greek commercial cities, but also in a number of Jewish settlements, particularly in Alexandria. We have already pointed out the importance of the Alexandrian Jewry in the history of medicine. Its importance in the development of philosophy is equally considerable.

Their respect for science and their desire to provide the

[4] *Ibid.,* p. 207.

scholar with an existence free from material care distinguished the Jews of the Middle Ages as mentally far superior to their barbarous environment. The Church was one of the communities, besides the Jews, which maintained alive the remnants of ancient civilisation in the midst of the Christian-Teutonic barbarism, and for this the Church has been not a little praised. But little attention has been given to the fact that the Church was practising a mental selection of the most dubious kind. In the Jewish families marriage and parenthood on the part of the most intelligent were assiduously encouraged.[5] The Catholic Church absorbed the most intelligent elements of the Christian families and doomed them to celibacy, forbade them to reproduce. This was equivalent to the precise opposite of the Jewish process of selection; the Church was practising a breeding of the most stupid, of course only during the period in which it served as the goal of the most intelligent men in the nation.

[5] This condition finally attained absurd dimensions among the Jews of Poland. In the section of his *Geschichte der neueren Philosophie* that deals with the Jewish philosopher Maimon (born 1754, died 1800), Kuno Fischer says:

"Among the Polish Jews the Talmudists and rabbis enjoyed the greatest prestige. Every family regarded it as a matter of pride to have a scholar of this type among its members, and if none of its sons was a Talmudist, effort was made to secure a son-in-law to embellish the family with such a connection. Young Talmudists were very much in demand as good matches. . . . Salomon Maimon had attained the third (supreme) degree in the Talmudic learning at the age of nine. . . . He was married before attaining the age of eleven. He was a husband in his eleventh year, a father in his fourteenth year." (Section v, pp. 120, 121.)

ARE THE JEWS A RACE?

Lecky, in his *Rise and Influence of the Spirit of Rationalism in Europe,* describes in glowing words the enthusiasm of the Jews for learning:

"While those around them were groveling in the darkness of besotted ignorance; while juggling miracles and lying relics were the themes on which all Europe was expatiating; while the intellect of Christendom, enthralled by countless superstitions, had sunk into a deadly torpor, in which all love of enquiry and all search for truth were abandoned, the Jews were still pursuing the path of knowledge, amassing learning, and stimulating progress with the same unflinching constancy that they manifested in their faith. They were the most skilful physicians, the ablest financiers, and among the most profound philosophers; while they were only second to the Moors in the cultivation of natural science. They were also the chief interpreters to Western Europe of Arab learning. But their most important service, and that with which we are now most especially concerned, was in sustaining commercial activity. For centuries they were almost its only representatives." [6]

Such were the circumstances under which the mental character of Judaism developed—and not from its "race" —whatever that may mean—but from the historical peculiarity of its social evolution. Precisely this historical evolution imparted to the Jews those qualities needed by capitalism, those qualities most conducive to success under

[6] W. E. H. Lecky, *History of the Rise and Influence of the Spirit of Rationalism in Europe,* New York, 1910, vol. ii, p. 103.

capitalism. The capitalist mode of production is predominantly urban in character; it concentrates the mass of the population in cities, makes the provinces economically dependent on the cities. It transforms all of production into commodities production, makes all of production dependent on the trade in commodities. It abolishes the handicraft routine, and replaces it by the application of science to all fields.

Therefore that section of the population will make itself most felt within capitalism whose faculties have been best adapted to urban life, to trade, to scientific labour: this means the Jews.

Of course, Sombart explains the capitalist spirit as well as the power of mental abstraction found among the Jews not on the basis of their urban life, nor of their commercial activity, but as due to the—cattle-breeding practised by the nomads of the desert who were among the ancestors of the Jews thousands of years ago!

"Out of the boundless desert, out of the supervision of flocks, arises capitalism in contrast to the old established economic order. The management of herds has no definitely limited domain, no clearly defined field of activity, for the field of cattle-breeding is unlimited; its practice may be destroyed overnight, or may grow ten-fold in the course of a few years."

Sombart does not explain how he accomplishes the miracle of causing a herd of cattle to grow ten-fold in the course of a few years; and yet such a revelation would be very valuable as an aid to overcoming the high price of meat. Furthermore, Sombart appears to regard pasture —in the wilderness—as unlimited, as well as the fodder furnished by it, which manifestly must also grow ten-fold in the course of a few years.

This new history of the origin of capitalism continues:

"Here (in the wilderness) alone, in the cattle-breeding economy—never in the sphere of agriculture—could the idea of gain strike root. Here only could economy be adapted naturally to an *unlimited increase* of the number of products."

In other words, the idea of unlimited increase, in other words, of unlimited fruitfulness, could only arise in the most unfruitful wildernesses, never in the most fruitful agricultural countries. The sandy desert is the indicated soil for the production of cattle and cattle-fodder in unlimited quantities.

But the desert not only creates the possibility of an unlimited increase of products, but the nomadic mode of pasturing pursued in the desert also creates the *impulse* to increase "possessions" beyond all limits, without regard to whether they are needed or not. Karl Marx supposed that the boundless proportions attained by the desire for accumulating a hoard, for collecting gold and silver, were a result of the production of commodities. But Sombart knows better. It was not the production of commodities, but the fact that oxen and cows produce calves, that created the boundless impulse—in the desert—of accumulating

142

hoards in cattle, of multiplying one's holdings in cattle ten-fold in the course of a few years, without asking for a moment whether this increased quantity can be put to any use, in other words, for the mere pleasure of counting the number of heads of cattle:

"Here only was it possible for the conception to arise that the abstract quantity of commodities and not the quality of utility is the dominant category of economic life. Here, for the first time, counting was resorted to in economic life. But the elements of rationalism also penetrated into the economic life, owing to nomad habits, which thus (!) become the father of capitalism in almost every respect. Again we find an immensely increased illumination for our understanding of the close relation between capitalism and Judaism, the latter here appearing as the connecting link between the former and nomadism."[7]

The "immensely increased illumination" which we find here serves only to illuminate the boundless fertility of the wilderness of our professor's imagination.

[7] *Die Juden und das Wirtschaftsleben*, pp. 425, 426.

CHAPTER VII

THE ASSIMILATION OF THE JEWS

THE mental race traits of the Jews are said to be of such nature as to constitute a profound and impassable gulf between them and all other races. On examination, this information resolves itself into the fact that the great mass of the Jews has constituted for two thousand years an exclusive, hereditary caste of urban merchants, financiers, intellectuals, including some artisans, and has developed, by practice and accumulation from generation to generation, more and more of the traits peculiar to all these strata, as opposed to the peasant masses of the rest of the population.

The Jews have always been distinguished from the latter since the termination of the existence of the Jewish state; they have always seemed strangers to the rest of the population, a condition encouraged in the Middle Ages by the fact that each vocation within the city was always concentrated in a certain quarter of the city. Within this quarter, if several races were represented, each of the races had its specific section. In addition, in the case of the Jews, we also have the peculiarity of their religion and their rite, all of which are matters that have nothing to do with race traits. But while the Jews may always have appeared

144

foreign, they were not always treated as enemies. Whether the Jews were regarded favourably or not depended entirely on the needs and conditions of the country in which they lived. The opposition which is frequently represented as a natural race hostility was determined by very mutable economic circumstances.

Wherever there was need of merchants or financiers, or intellectuals in general, and wherever the native supply of such elements was insufficient, the Jew was welcome. Such was the case in the Christian empires of Western and Northern Europe in the centuries after the migration of nations, in other words, at precisely the period when "Germanism" must have been in evidence in its purest form. Cities then developed with the utmost difficulty. The Jews were welcome as a means of invigorating the economic life of the cities.

"At all points where this formation of cities is going on, where an urban community is developing out of the former *castellum* of the Romans, the Jews contributed a decisive element by bringing trade within the walls. This is expressed in a truly classic manner in the words in which Bishop Rüdiger of Speyer opens his Charter to the Jews in the year 1084: 'Desiring to make a city out of the village of Speyer, I have admitted the Jews. . . .' The Bishop not only points out that the Jews enjoy the same rights in other cities, such as complete trade privileges, property in land, local autonomy, but adds also: 'I have thought to multiply one thousand times the honour of our

145

city by gathering the Jews within its walls.' This Charter
was expanded into a general privilege by Emperor
Henry IV. The Archbishop of Cologne in his Charter of
1252 says: 'We believe that it will redound not a little to
our prosperity and honour if the Jews who entrust themselves to our support and who—hoping for our protection
and our favour—submit to our rule—may actually enjoy
this protection.' " [1]

The Jews of Cologne obtained not only autonomy within
the Jewish quarter but full rights of citizenship and admission to parish offices. Thus, G. L. von Maurer quotes a
document dating from "about 1200", in which a Jew
named Egeberth is appointed as Alderman of the Parish of
Saint Lorenz.[2] But von Maurer is obliged to admit that
the Jews did not hold this favourable position except "for
a time". "On the whole, they had greater privileges in
the earlier period than in the later." [3]

For the Jews in Christendom fared somewhat as the Germans in Bohemia. As long as they were needed in order
to develop and encourage the growth of cities and in order
to invigorate trade, they were welcome. When the cities
began to develop a class of native financiers, traders, and
artisans, the imported foreigners, once they had become
established, were no longer regarded as a welcome assistance, but as an undesirable competition, as "undesirable

[1] Zollschan, *Das Rassenproblem,* pp. 351, 353.
[2] *Geschichte der Städteverfassung,* vol. ii, p. 232.
[3] *Op. cit.,* p. 230.

aliens". The population suddenly bethought itself that some difference or other, of religious or other nature—the distinctions between races had not yet been invented in those "dark" ages—constituted an opposition obliging one to persecute the foreigners. While the Jews had been sought for in Western Europe down into the Thirteenth Century, every effort was made from that time on to make life unbearable for them, to abridge their rights; they were maltreated, plundered, and driven out, if not actually slain. Wherever a wretched existence is still possible for them, their activity is restricted in every possible way. They are prevented from engaging in large-scale commercial enterprises, are forbidden to own land, to practise a trade. Nothing is left to them but the trade of usury and a petty huckstery and colportage. The haggling Jew as a type of the Jewish "race" is a product of Christian charity.

We may mention—merely as a curiosity—the fact that it was during this period of the most intense persecutions that the Jews were forbidden to visit disorderly houses. Thus Queen Jeanne I issued such a prohibition in 1347 for the City of Avignon. This pious and virtuous potentate reserved the privilege of visiting the bordello to Christians. By reason of its enduring into the Sixteenth Century, this privilege was transformed into a greater privilege on the part of Christians to acquire syphilis.[4] Perhaps as a

---

[4] Lecky, *op cit.*, vol. ii, pp. 100, 101, especially the footnotes.

measure of compensatory justice, Christians were forbidden to obtain treatment from Jewish physicians.

The reader will observe that the health of the Christians was not enhanced by the persecutions of the Jews.

The rise of the modern state at first brought no alleviation to the Jews. To be sure, the state's strong police power considerably abridged irregular plundering—the plunderings of its subjects now became the monopoly of the state, and were applied, with the aid of its organized power, in the form of taxes.

On the other hand, this same state authority showed itself to be very suspicious toward all autonomous bodies. Any independence, any deviation from the mode of thought prescribed by the state power was tabooed and often subject to cruel penalties. Thus, the religion of the ruling monarch was considered to determine also the religious feeling of all his subjects. Where the Jews were weak and not numerous, their religious peculiarities might still be tolerated. Where they constituted a power, they were now most brutally maltreated by the state authority, frequently driven out of the country, as was the case particularly in Spain and Portugal. Hundreds of thousands were banished from the former country in 1492, and hundreds of thousands of others converted to Christianity by force. A similar compulsion was carried out in Portugal shortly thereafter.

It was not until industrial capital became strong that the general position became more favourable to the Jews.

THE ASSIMILATION OF THE JEWS

Industrial capital arises not only in opposition to feudal landlordism and to guild handicraft and financial capital. The latter aim at attaining privileges from the state, while industrial capital seeks to maintain free competition within its ranks. The greater the competition among merchants and those who hold the power to grant credits, the better will industry flourish. It was in the interest of industry to permit Jewish traders and Jewish financiers to compete with Christians, to abolish the barriers which kept out the former. This attitude was fully in keeping with the general tendency to abolish mediæval guilds. The ghetto was one of the mediæval corporations. It had to go, in the interest of a speedy evolution of capitalism; though it continued, in some cities, into the Modern Era, its fate was sealed.

But industrial capitalism is distinguished from the artisanry of the Feudal Era not only by reason of the fact that it is obliged to break down all the guild barriers, but also because of the fact that it substitutes an application of science for the traditional routine. Simultaneously there ensues a necessary expansion of the newspaper system. For these reasons, as well as for others, the enumeration of which would take us too far afield, the demand for intellectuals of every variety increased. But the supply offered by the feudal state was comparatively low. The Church still absorbed so many intellectuals as to constitute a serious interference with the demands of learning and capital. It became absolutely necessary for the new and rising mode of production to liberate the Jewish intelli-

gentsia and to cut off the uninterrupted blood-letting practised by the Church, particularly the Catholic Church, with
its commandment of celibacy, on the non-Jewish intelligentsia.

In all these efforts, industrial capitalism found itself
impeded more and more not only by feudal landlordism,
by guild handicraft, by the Church, by the privileged strata
among the intellectuals, by the commercial organisations,
by high finance, but also by the power of the state itself,
which was ruled by these classes, and which was naturally
applying the means of its authority in the interests of
these classes.

Only by overthrowing this authority could the path be
cleared for a most speedy evolution of the new mode of
production. In this process, industrial capitalism found
allies only in the lower classes, in the proletariat and in
the peasantry, as well as in those strata of the petty bourgeoisie and the intelligentsia which were not among the
privileged classes and which could advance only by means
of an elimination of all privileges. Thus modern democracy arose with its pronouncement of the equality of all
creatures in human form. The natural consequence was
an effort to emancipate Judaism, and also—on the other
hand—an alliance between the energetic, aggressive elements of Judaism and revolution. Only through revolution could Judaism be liberated.

The negative, destructive, critical spirit which is said to
be a natural trait of the Jewish race is in reality the neces-

sary outcome of the social and political situation of Judaism, which excluded it from all the advantages of existing society, and made the Jews feel their disadvantages most keenly. If this spirit is a race trait, it is among the invariable race traits of every oppressed and exploited class during such period of oppression and exploitation.

The liberation of the Jews was realised in the great French Revolution and in its minor successors. It was heralded by an increasing tolerance for the Jews in the more advanced capitalist states, first in Holland, then in England, beginning with the Seventeenth Century, a change which brought many Spanish and Portuguese Jewish or pseudo-Christian capitalists to those states. Finally, the Jew obtained equal rights with all other citizens. Thereupon he began to rise rapidly in capitalistic society, to whose needs he had become so perfectly adapted, in trade, in banking, in journalism, in medicine, in jurisprudence. But simultaneously there also began the Jew's adaptation to non-Jewish society, his *assimilation.*

This process was apparent in his language; the modern Jew no longer speaks with a Jewish accent. Then it ensued in his rite: the dietary laws and commandments for the celebration of festivals, which once separated the Jew from the non-Jew, constituting such a profound gulf between them, now cease to govern the Jew entirely. More and more Jews leave their religious community. Zollschan cites an estimate made by Licencié de la Roy, to the effect that more than two hundred thousand Jews were baptised in the

151

course of the Nineteenth Century, not including conversions to dissenting groups or the baptisms of children of mixed marriages. And this tendency to conversions from Judaism is on the increase. In Vienna, the annual number of conversions was as follows:

	Conversions from Judaism	No. of Jews per Conversion
1886-1890	330	359
1896-1900	511	288
1900	607	240
1906	643	...

After giving these data, together with many others, Zollschan draws the following inference:

"If we recapitulate all this material, we shall find a considerable increase in the number of Jewish baptisms in western countries. Judaism in Austria (not counting Galicia) is losing more than 2 per 1,000 of its adherents annually; in Germany, at least 1 per 1,000; in Hungary, about ¾ per 1,000, to Christianity. On the other hand, the huge Jewish zone in Russia and Galicia is maintaining its ground against Christian influences and is suffering only slight abrasions." [5]

Far greater than the number of Jews who abandon their religious affiliation is the number of those who, though they remain in it, nevertheless completely relinquish their religious practice and their religious mode of thought. Of

[5] Zollschan, *op. cit.*, p. 475.

course, the same process is simultaneously going on among the great majority of the non-Jewish urban population, who also, by force of habit, still remain within the field of the traditional religious organisations, without having the slightest share in the religious life of these organisations. The religious assimilation of the Jews in Western Europe is making rapid progress, not so much because the Jews are accepting the Christian faith or the Christians accepting the Jewish faith, as because both parties are succumbing to the same unbelief and to the same religious indifferentism.

This finds its expression also in the number of *mixed marriages*, which is increasing rapidly. Thus, the number of mixed marriages between Jews and non-Jews in Prussia was:

Average for the Years	Percentage of Purely Jewish Marriages
1875-1884	10.1
1885-1894	12.4
1895-1899	16.9
1905	23.6
1906	23.3
1907	25.6

In the large cities with a numerous Jewish population, the number of mixed marriages is either already very large, or is rapidly increasing.

The figures for a few of these cities are given below.

City	Average for the Years	Number of Mixed Marriages Between Jews and Non-Jews Given as a Percentage of Purely Jewish Marriages
Berlin	1901-1904	35.4
	1905	44.4
Frankfort on	1905	22.5
the Main	1906	26.0
	1907	19.6
	1908	30.7
Hamburg	1903-1905	49.5
Amsterdam	1899	8.1
	1900	8.8
	1901	11.3
	1902	13.6
	1903	20.1

The figures for Amsterdam especially show a rapid increase in mixed marriages.

In Italy, France, England, and the United States, there are no religious statistics. Zollschan sadly observes that in these countries, in which the Jews have the fullest freedom, "the process of dissolution of the native Jewry is proceeding at full speed".[6] In the Jewish families of Italy which belong to the higher social classes he says it has "almost become a rule to marry their children only to Christians".

The figures from Trieste, until recently an Austrian city, but which has always had a predominantly Italian population, point in the same direction. In Austria, mixed

[6] Zollschan, *op. cit.*, p. 477.

marriages were subject to considerable limitation, being permitted only between Jews and unbelievers. And marriages in which both the Jewish and the Christian party were without religious affiliation were not considered as mixed marriages.

In spite of all this, the number of mixed marriages in Trieste, as a percentage of purely Jewish marriages, was as follows:

1877-1890	33.3
1891-1895	38.5
1896-1899	41.6
1900-1903	61.4

To be sure, this is in the country of "black" Italians. But—oh, horror!—in the land of the noblest blonds, the "black-blond mix-up", in spite of all the offence this may give to Sombart's holiest emotions, is proceeding most abominably. In Copenhagen, the number of mixed marriages between Jews and non-Jews, expressed as a percentage of the purely Jewish marriages, was as follows:

1880-1889	55.8
1889-1899	68.7
1900-1905	82.9

Accordingly, Zollschan declares:

"It is apparent that the Jewish population of Denmark has not increased in the sixty years from 1840 to 1901, but has decreased absolutely and even more, relatively. In 1840, 0.3 per cent. of the total population was still Jewish; in 1901, only 0.14 per cent. The proportion of Jews had therefore decreased by more than one-half. The reason is not only the comparatively small number of children, but chiefly the numerous mixed marriages by means of which the Danish Jews are being gradually absorbed by the non-Jewish population." [7]

The examples of Italy and Denmark go to show how correct were the calculations of those champions of Jewish emancipation who expected that it would result in a complete absorption of the Jews by the races among which they lived. Zollschan is right; it is only in the ghetto, in a condition of compulsory exclusion from their environment, and under political pressure, deprived of their rights and surrounded by hostility, that the Jews can maintain themselves among other peoples. They will dissolve, unite with their environment and disappear, where the Jew is regarded and treated as a free man and as an equal.

There now remains only one possible source of a new lease of life for Judaism and therefore also for the "Jewish peril", namely, the peril that non-Jews will be forced out by Jews in the struggle of capitalist competition. This new lease of life for the "Jewish peril" may come from anti-Semitism.

[7] Zollschan, *op. cit.*, p. 478.

CHAPTER VIII

ANTI-SEMITISM

INDUSTRIAL capitalism, by means of its union with the revolutionary portions of the intelligentsia, had put down the elements opposing it. The result was a form of the state organisation which favoured an extremely rapid growth of industrial capital but also permitted the disadvantages involved in the latter for the petty bourgeoisie and the proletariat to express themselves most clearly. Sooner or later each of these two classes turned its back on bourgeois democracy or liberalism—the earlier, the lower was the degree of revolutionary energy developed by the latter in the period of its rise, and the less profound was therefore its spiritual control of the masses of the people, which depended in turn on the stage reached in the general economic evolution and therefore by the proletarian movement as a whole. The later the introduction of the bourgeois-democratic opposition and revolution, the greater is the internal resistance it feels by reason of its fear of the proletariat. As we travel from west to east, from England to Russia, we find liberalism entering later and later on the political arena. We find liberalism therefore growing weaker and weaker, being less and less capable of maintaining the proletarians and petty bourgeois in a state of dependence on itself, and the earlier do both these elements cut loose from liberalism, until finally, in Russia, we reach a stage where the proletariat, as well as the petty bourgeoisie, has already been separated from liberalism before it enters upon the political struggle.

But the opposition to liberalism assumes, as is well known, quite a different form among the proletariat than among the petty bourgeoisie. Both find their social position in capitalistic society intolerable. But, in the case of the proletariat, the achievements of democracy and of capitalist economy are the presupposition for its own liberation. The proletariat does not seek to neutralise these achievements of democracy, but rather to annex them, to utilize them in its own struggle.

The petty bourgeoisie would have as much to gain from socialism as the proletariat, but only a portion of its members is able to rise, through its political leadership, to the recognition of this fact. The conditions of its existence at the present time depend on private property in the means of production and on the exploitation of wage-labourers, particularly of the weakest of all wage-labourers, particularly women and children. In this process, it encounters the resistance of the proletariat, and is made to contrast sharply with the proletariat and its socialist tendencies.

Considerable portions of the petty bourgeoisie, turning from liberalism, do not seek their salvation in advancing beyond liberalism, but rather feel themselves obliged to retrace their steps, to become politically and economically reactionary, in which process they find allies in the powers that had been surmounted by liberalism.

Of course, they cannot turn back the wheel of history. No doubt, capitalism is changing. With the issues of stock shares and the expansion of the banks, industrial capital is concentrating more and more and beginning to coincide with financial capital. The tendencies of the primitive financial and trading capital to eliminate competition by private monopoly are again becoming manifest. The political reaction may for a time be encouraged by such measures, but economically capitalism is thus being pushed to the extreme. The petty bourgeoisie gains nothing by such methods.

Powerless to combat capitalism as a whole, it has no other recourse than to fight individual, partial manifestations of capitalism and thus to join the political reaction, of which it expects, of course in vain, an economic reaction also.

In this situation, it finds a fruitful soil for the reawakening of anti-Semitic tendencies. The battle against capital as a whole seems hopeless. But the conflict with Judaism, with Jewish capital, which is so unpleasantly felt by many a non-Jewish capitalist, seems to afford better prospects of success.

But not only proletarians and petty bourgeois turn their backs on liberalism, which has not fulfilled their expectations, and feel themselves threatened by the rising tide of Judaism. The vanguard of liberalism had been composed of intellectuals. As long as they occupied an exceptional position, as long as they were an unusual curiosity, their position was favourable; but this condition gradually subsided in the course of the Nineteenth Century. An overproduction of intellectuals began to make itself felt, for which there were many reasons, not the least among which was the decline of the petty bourgeoisie, which is sending its sons—now even its daughters—to the university, or, if the means are not available for this, at least to commercial and trade schools, in order to enable them to make their way as clerks or as independent mental workers, since handicraft and petty trade no longer afford these opportunities. Again we find, in the most varied fields, that it is the Jews who advance most quickly. Therefore, among non-Jewish intellectuals and clerks also, those who are incapable of accepting socialism, which would put an end to all the ills of a competitive society, become quite accessible to anti-Semitic influences, which are an expression of their own discontent with life.

Thus, since the 'seventies of the Nineteenth Century, we again find movements in rather extensive sections of the population of Germany, Austria, France, etc., which favour a political disfranchisement, and a legal restriction or at least a social boycott of the Jews. Aspirations which unite with the anti-Jewish hatred on the part of narrow-minded circles and with the contempt for the Jews on the part of feudal arrogance, to both of which they impart renewed strength.

Sombart manages to justify to himself the reduction of the rights of Jews in the army and at the universities:

"The practice in all of Germany at present, in filling the professorships at the universities, as well as in admissions to the position of *Privatdozent*, is practically not to exclude Jews on principle, but to place certain restrictions on their admission or election. *This may be regrettable in the interest of an officially certified science, for it is always equivalent to an injury to the scientific performance of a serious institution of learning if of two competitors the more stupid is chosen for a certain position. But is it possible to consider scientific interests alone, or even predominantly, in filling the positions of professors at a university?* Or, putting the question to fit our conditions: Would it be a conceivable and tolerable condition to have all the positions of *Dozent* and Professors at the universities filled by Jews—baptised or not baptised—that makes no difference? Since the Jews are on the average so much brighter and so much more industrious than we, this might be equivalent to completely handing over the positions of university instruction to the Jews. . . . Perhaps the universities will suffer more from such restrictions than the Jews themselves. . . . But in the long run, it is better thus." [1]

Well then: learning suffers more from the existing con-

[1] Sombart, *Die Zukunft der Juden*, pp. 82, 83.

dition of keeping out the Jews, but nevertheless it is "in the long run, better thus", for the universities are "after all" not institutions in which "the interests of science alone, or even predominantly, may be considered". They are not the seat of the high goddess of science, but merely stalls for the needed milch cattle, institutions which must provide so and so many posts for so and so many aspirants coming from good families. Therefore it would not be right to permit the Jews to take possession of the whole business. "But in the long run, it is better thus."

And how about the army? Here, it really appears that the officers will not tolerate Jews among their number and for so "clever a man" as Sombart that is quite sufficient.

"The traditions followed in the army are, after all, anti-Semitic traditions. . . . This is a fact that may be regretted but which cannot be eliminated because of this regret, a fact *with which* every clever man will have to reckon." [2]

All persons who take off their hats to any obstacle that would require a greater exertion of energy than mere "regretting" apparently seem "clever" to Sombart.

We should therefore not be astonished to find Sombart formulating his "programme" on the Jewish question "briefly" as follows:

"The nations give their (the nations'?) Jewish fellow-citizens full equality of rights, and the Jews will surely be intelligent and tactful enough not to demand a full exercise

[2] *Ibid.*, pp. 85, 86.

of this equality of rights at every point and to the fullest possible extent." [3]

This "intelligence", which at one and the same time offers to both the Jews and their opponents everything they ask, to the former of course only in the protasis, to the latter in the apodosis, is really matchless and baffles all attempts to parallel it.

In spite of all the anti-Semitism, of all the restrictions and disabilities of the Jews, the rise of Judaism, together— of course—with its dissolution because of desertions from the faith and because of mixed marriages, is still in progress. The data we have already given on this subject are all taken from the period of the renaissance of anti-Semitism.

If, in spite of this fact, the effects of assimilation have been apparently brought to a standstill, and Judaism is not losing ground as a distinct racial group, we may ascribe this to the movement that has recently been gaining greatly in popularity among the Jews of Eastern Europe.

We have seen above how the persecutions of the Jews precisely in the days of humanism and precisely in the most enlightened sections of Europe made existence almost impossible for the Jews, who fled to the East, to Poland, and Turkey. In these barbarous countries they were tolerated precisely for the reason that they were barbarous countries which were in need of a city population. In their

[3] *Ibid.*, p. 87.

capacity as strangers, being tolerated merely, they must have been particularly welcome in the eyes of those in power, who would necessarily regard with disfavour a *strong* urban bourgeoisie, which would have limited their own power.

In the regions then belonging to Poland and Turkey, in Hungary, Rumania, Poland proper, and the western portion of Russia, the Jews gathered from all portions of Europe, particularly from Germany. The Spanish Jews, for the most part, sought the southern sections of European Turkey (Saloniki). The legal, and for the most part even the economic, situation of the Jews in Turkey, is at present still the best in the world.[4]

Most of the Jews in the world have concentrated in these regions. According to figures given by Nawratzki, the number of Jews in the world immediately before the war was between 12,500,000 and 13,000,000.[5] Trieksch gives a higher estimate; [6] he makes their total number 14,500,000 in 1914.

Nawratzki assigns 6,000,000 Jews to Russia, 1,000,000 to Galicia and the Bukowina, 900,000 to Hungary, 300,000

[4] W. W. Kaplun-Kogan, *Die Wanderbewegungen der Juden*, Bonn, 1913, p. 46. Valuable statistical material may also be found in the essay of I. M. Rubinow, *The Economic Condition of the Jews in Russia*, Bulletin of the Bureau of Labour, Washington, D. C., 1907. *Cf.* also the series of articles, *Die ökonomische Lage des jüdischen Proletariats in Russland*, *Die Neue Zeit*, vol. xxiv, part 1, p. 231 *et seq.*

[5] C. Nawratzki, *Die jüdische Kolonisation Palästinas*, München, 1914, pp. xvi, 538.

[6] *Palästina und die Juden*, Berlin, 1919, p. 46.

to Rumania, 200,000 to European Turkey, while Trieksch
assigns 7,000,000 to Russia, 2,300,000 to Austria, 300,000
to Rumania, and 400,000 to Turkey.[7]

In other words, about 8,500,000-10,000,000 Jews in
round numbers were living in the domains of former Poland
and former Turkey. Those living in Great Britain (250,-
000-300,000) and America (2,300,000-2,500,000) have for
the most part migrated into those countries from the
former regions in comparatively recent days. This would
give a figure of from 11,000,000 to 13,000,000 living in
Eastern Europe, or coming from Eastern Europe, and of
not quite 2,000,000 Jews of every provenience in the rest
of the world.

They are found most densely settled in the regions of
former Poland, where they came directly from Germany or
by way of Germany, with the result that they have preserved to this day a peculiar language distinguishing them
from their Slavonic environment, the so-called Yiddish, a
corrupt German—the only Jewish population in the world
that has not assimilated the language of its environment.
It is in this Russian-Polish Jewish population that the
Jew's consciousness, or orthodoxy, has been most vigor-
ously and actively maintained.

Living together in such great numbers, they could not
remain a nation of merchants, usurers and intellectuals

[7] See also the estimates made by Israel Cohen, *Jewish Life in
Modern Times*, London, 1914, p. 345 *et seq.*, also the *World Almanac*
for 1926, p. 698.—TRANSLATOR.

alone. This was made all the less possible by the fact that the country in which they lived was not only economically backward when they settled there, but continued to remain so. The shifting of trade routes to India, once a land-route over Europe, later a sea-route, circumnavigating Africa, the discovery of America, the displacement of the economic centre of gravity of Europe to the coast of the Atlantic Ocean, retarded the development not only of Italy, but still more that of Poland and Turkey, and thus inaugurated the political decline and disintegration of those two countries. Under these circumstances, no strong capitalist industry could develop, and the intelligentsia also were cut off from their relations with the mental life of the rest of Europe and became entirely subordinate to the servants of the religious rite. The entire magnificent mental growth ensuing upon the Italian Renaissance did not exist for them. They remained living in the age of scholasticism, in the Jewish scholasticism of the Talmud. This species of intellectual ability was required only among the Jews, and the demand for any other kind of intelligence on the part of the non-Jewish community was very low. Therefore, a large portion of the Polish Jews turned to handicrafts, particularly to tailoring. In the Jewish pale, in other words, in that portion of the Russian Empire in which the great mass of the Jews were alone permitted to dwell, the Russian Census of 1897, which was the first and last census carried out by the Czarist Empire, gives the following occupational figures:

ANTI-SEMITISM

	Employed in Gainful Occupations Absolute Number		Percentages		Per Each 100 Non-Jews in the Same Category There Were
	Jews	Non-Jews	Jews	Non-Jews	Jews
Total population ..	1,428,835	9,854,054	100	100	14.5
Employed in Industry	518,075	1,132,264	36	11.5	46
Employed in the Garment Industry	235,993	222,764	16.5	2.0	106
Employed in Commerce	450,427	108,499	31.5	1.7	415
Employed in Grain and Cattle Trade	202,016	57,485	14	0.6	351

These figures are those of our own times.[8] In former days, the Jews constituted the great mass of the urban, commercial, and, in many cases, even the industrial population in the regions we are discussing.

After the Crimean War, and during the era of liberalism which ensued upon it, a fully developed western capitalism suddenly forced its way into those economically backward countries. Its first effect was that of immensely increasing the money needs of the state, its indebtedness, but also its tax burdens. At a single stroke, the natural economy of the peasant was transformed into a commod-

[8] I take them from a book of L. Hersch, *Le Juif errant d'aujourd'hui, Etude sur l'émigration des Israélites de l'Europe orientale aux Etats-Unis de l'Amérique*, Paris, 1913, p. 191. This book appeared practically at the same time with the above mentioned book of Kaplun-Kogan, on the migrations of the Jews. Both books partly treat the same subject, with the same material, and arrive at similar conclusions, thus giving support to each other. Hersch goes more into statistical details, while Kaplun-Kogan's treatment is more comprehensive. I have found both very useful in the present study.

167

ities economy, which under the given circumstances did not improve the operation of his farm, but rather ruined it by reason of a more and more intensified robbing of the soil. An increasing proportion of the country population was driven into the cities. As early as in the census of 1897, of the 14,300,000 non-Jewish inhabitants of the cities, 7,300,000 had come from the peasantry.[9] The influx from city to country has since assumed much greater proportions. But in the cities, these persons found no quickly growing industry which might have been able to absorb them, nor did the deteriorating peasants offer any adequate market for such an industry. Competition grew among artisans and peddlers. The Jews were now oppressed more and more; their situation—never very brilliant—now became more and more hopeless. But the non-Jewish population also suffered; the frame of production was too small to accommodate all, and the mass of the population was too ignorant to seek or find a solution of these difficulties in a corresponding expansion of this frame, for the condition of economic backwardness was closely connected with the political backwardness, and any effort to alter the state authority was also connected with too many dangers. It was far less dangerous, far more convenient and simple to turn against that competition which was represented by the defenceless Jews.

The state authority itself, in its various organs, met these tendencies more than halfway. For it felt itself

[9] Hersch, *op. cit.*, p. 229.

168

threatened by the results of the economic revolution, even though the latter might for the present be engendering political opposition, not in the masses of the people, but only in the young men and women at the universities. The growing discontent was unmistakable; the heads of the state felt it necessary to ward it off, and the unhappy Jews were obliged to furnish a convenient lightning-rod.

The anti-Semitic tendencies in the upper and lower strata were strengthened by the fact that in Russia, more than anywhere else, the Jews had escaped assimilation by reason of their concentration in a single region. They differed greatly from the rest of the population, not only—as we have already seen—by their rigid adherence to their rite, to the dietary laws, the observing of holidays, the peculiarities of their language,[10] but also in their headdress. In Russia and the adjacent countries, more than anywhere else, the Jew has remained a foreigner among the people. Foreignness may be comic in its effect where it reveals only a difference, and is not associated with a social contradiction. But when the latter also is present, it makes the difference more striking and tangible, it produces inciting and embittering conditions.

Thus there arose after a short period of liberalism, and,

[10] As late as 1897, the Census of that year showed that 5,054,300 persons of Jewish faith gave "Yiddish" as their mother-tongue, while 161,505 gave another language. At the same time, we find 8,856 persons of non-Jewish faith setting down Yiddish as their mother-tongue, obviously converted Jews—but incompletely converted. *Cf.* Rubinow, *The Economic Condition of the Jews in Russia,* p. 488.

beginning with the 'eighties of the Nineteenth Century, a period of a most savage and intensifying anti-Semitism, of increasing maltreatments of the Jews by their environment, and of a progressive disfranchisement. After 1882, the Jews were limited to a pale of settlement embracing only four per cent. of the area of the Russian Empire. Only rich merchants, certain intellectuals, and certain master-artisans were permitted to settle outside the pale, and within it, they were permitted to live only in the cities. All the Jews who had settled in the country districts were forced into the cities beginning with 1882, and many who had ventured outside of the pale of settlement during the liberal era were again forced back into it.

Among those congested in this area, a terrible period of distress ensued. The pogroms were bad enough. Worse were the devilish torments and extortions practised by the Russian authorities; worst of all was the material distress.

In this terrible situation only the bravest are courageous enough to fight for a better lot. Of the others, all who have any means of doing so, and any prospect of obtaining employment elsewhere, resort to emigration; industrial workers therefore emigrated more than petty tradesmen. Particularly marked is the emigration in the overcrowded vocations. According to the census of 1897, there were 147,435 Jews employed as tailors in the pale of settlement. From 1899 to 1910, 15,396 members of this trade emigrated to the United States from the pale of settlement each year; in other words, 10.5 per cent. annually. On the other hand, the average for shoemakers was only 1960 per year, or 2.7 per cent. The garment industry was predominantly still a domestic industry, producing for the local requirements, while in the shoemaking industry factory production was rapidly growing, and filled a market over all Russia.[11] The Jewish immigration to America was more numerous than to any other country. From 1881 to 1912, the total Jewish immigration to the United States amounted to 2,258,146 persons; from 1899 to 1912, to 1,246,260 persons. The total immigration of Jews from 1881 to 1898 was 1,011,886, of which 526,122, or more than half, came from Russia. From 1899 to 1911, the total number of Jewish immigrants was 1,165,665, of which 831,001, or three-quarters, came from Russia.

The Jewish emigration from Russia to the countries of Western Europe was far smaller than the above figures. According to Ruppin's figures, the following numbers of Jews emigrated from 1881 to 1908.

	From Russia	From Austria	From Germany	From Other Countries	Total
To England...........	150,000	10,000	20,000	10,000	190,000
To Germany..........	15,000	25,000	......	......	40,000
To France............	30,000	10,000	......	10,000	50,000
To Belgium...........	5,000	......	......	5,000	10,000

In the case of Germany and Austria, internal migrations of Jews from east to west were of greater importance. This was a portion of the general migration so character-

[11] Hersch, *op. cit.*, p. 240.

istic of capitalism, namely, the migration from country to city, from agricultural districts to industrial districts. The process was accentuated by the economic conditions of the Polish sections of those countries, which in Germany and Austria, as well as in Russia, though not to so great a degree nor in such brutal forms as the latter, were making a portion of the agricultural population unnecessary, which surplus population flowed in part into the cities and supplanted the Jews or emigrated together with the Jews.

In the Province of Posen (Prussia) there were still 76,757 Jews in 1849, but only 26,512 in 1910! The provinces of East Prussia, West Prussia, Pomerania and Posen, together, had still 116,075 Jews in 1871, and only 62,355 in 1910. This migration was directed chiefly toward Berlin. Within the city limits of Berlin and the Province of Brandenburg, the Jewish population grew from 47,489 persons in 1871, to 151,356 persons in 1910.

Similarly, the number of Jews in Vienna increased from 73,222 in 1880 to 175,318 in 1910, an increase of 139 per cent., while the total Jewish population of Austria increased only 30 per cent. in the same period. In Russian Poland, Warsaw included in 1893 only 13.8 per cent. of the Jewish population of Poland (168,677 Jews, of a total Jewish population of 1,224,652), while in 1909 it included 16.1 per cent. (281,754 persons, of a total Jewish population of 1,747,655); in 1910, the Jewish population of Warsaw amounted to 308,488. The Jewish population of

Lodz tripled in the same period, increasing from 37,106 to 92,558 persons.[12]

Almost all the Jewish immigrants entering France gathered in Paris; those entering England, in London; while the majority of those headed for the United States remained in New York, which now counts more than 1,000,-000 Jews.[13]

The mere fact of its concentration in a few great metropolises necessarily has brought the Jewish population more and more into the foreground. This condition is further accentuated by the fact that the immigrant Jews are far more sharply distinct from their new environment and appear much more foreign in it than do the Jews who have lived in the same environment for many years.

The new great migratory movement of the Jews is of entirely different type from that of former days. Formerly, the Jews emigrated to countries of lower, or at least not higher, culture. Now we find backward Jewish masses flowing to countries at a high stage of development, together with Irishmen, Southern Italians, Poles and Ruthenians, or Chinese. To be sure, the Polish Jews in their homeland are superior in education to their environment,

[12] Hersch, op. cit., pp. 172, 309.

[13] According to the estimate of the American Jewish Year Book (1925-26), there were, in 1920, 1,643,012 Jews in the City of New York. Of the Jews, the Borough of Manhattan shelters 657,101; Brooklyn, 604,380; The Bronx, 278,169; Queens, 86,194; Richmond, 17,168. About 29 per cent. of the New York City population is Jewish, by the above estimate; they comprise 38 per cent. of the inhabitants of the Bronx.—TRANSLATOR.

173

which is one of the causes preventing their assimilation with the non-Jewish population. But as compared with Western Europeans or Americans, they are on a lower level.

The Russian census of 1897 recorded among male Jews above the age of 10, 33.4 per cent. of illiterates, while among the non-Jewish families of the same age-group, even as many as 63.4 per cent. were illiterate! But of course it must be remembered that the total population of Russia showed an illiteracy among males above the age of 10 of no less than 61.3 per cent., and among females of no less than 83 per cent! Immigrants entering the United States are examined as to their ability to read and write. In these tests, the Jews showed better percentages than were displayed in the Russian census of 1897. This may be due partly to the fact that the American figures I am using are of later date than the Russian (1910,[14] as compared with 1897), and also to the fact that only adults were considered in the American figures ; perhaps also because the most ignorant would be most likely to remain at home. Furthermore, the American figures included all Jewish immigrants, not only those coming from Russia. Nevertheless, the Jews appear from these figures to be far beyond other peoples in the matter of literacy as is shown by the following table from Hersch's book.[15]

[14] Hersch, *op. cit.*, p. 91.

[15] Jewish immigration to the United States has been greatly reduced, together with most other immigration, as a result of recent restrictive legislation.—TRANSLATOR.

174

ANTI-SEMITISM

Illiterates per 1,000 Adult Immigrants

Scandinavians	4	Slovaks	240
Scotch	7	*Jews*	260
English	11	Greeks	264
Finns	13	Rumanians	340
Czechs	17	Poles	354
Irish	25	Croatians and Slovenes	361
Dutch	44	Russians	384
Germans [16]	52	Bulgarians and Serbs	409
French	63	Lithuanians	489
North Italians	112	Ruthenians	534
Magyars	114	Southern Italians	539
Spaniards	145	Portuguese	682

Only Eastern and Southern Slavs, Southern Italians and Portuguese show a higher percentage of illiteracy than the great majority of the immigrant Jews. This condition is a disgrace not to the races involved, but to their governments. The orthodox Jewish elements who flowed from the East to the highly developed West were quite backward. The first effect of this condition was to retard the process of assimilation on the part of the Jews of the West; a further effect was the reviving of anti-Semitism. The latter process was stimulated in two ways; in the first place, by the increased competition faced by intellectuals and traders; in the second place, by the more emphatically foreign aspect of the Jewish community. But anti-Semitism is no longer what it used to be. In former days, it was directed chiefly against capitalist exploitation, of which the Jew was considered—in anti-Semitic countries—

[16] Including also Germans from Austria.

the most outstanding representative. Now it is more and more the proletarian Jew, the poor student, the poor peddler, the worker who works in his own house, who incurs the hostility of the anti-Semites. The times are passed when anti-Semitism might parade as a variety of socialism —"the socialism of the simple citizen of Vienna". Today, anti-Semitism is a phase of the struggle against the proletariat, and it is indeed the most cowardly and brutal of these phases; it has become "the socialist-baiting of the simple citizen of Vienna".

Meanwhile, a gap has opened up within Judaism itself; the wealthy and cultured Jews of the West, who have been almost assimilated, are in many cases unpleasantly affected by the new accession of their poor, ignorant "Yiddish" brothers from the East. They very often regard the latter with feelings that might be designated as an anti-Semitism within Judaism itself.

Formerly, one of the most prominent characteristics of the Jews had been the intimate solidarity prevailing within their own ranks. The constant persecutions had powerfully supported their inner cohesion, and this strong cohesion had become one of the most effective means of resisting persecution. Although frequently represented as a Jewish race trait, it is—like the rest of their alleged earmarks—only a product of the conditions of their life.

With every change in these conditions, there comes also a change in the "race trait". The feeling of solidarity on the part of the Western Jews has already been weakened considerably, because of—or perhaps in spite of—the fact that social anti-Semitism in the West (in Berlin, Paris, London, New York, and particularly in Vienna) has temporarily increased. Among Jewish capitalists who have risen to occupy dominant positions in the existing order, the feeling of Jewish solidarity is but rarely in evidence, and when expressed at all, it takes the form of charity. Such charity—in view of their rapidly increasing wealth—may assume large proportions, but it is extended only to the *mendicant*, not to the *fighting* Jewish proletariat.

The Jewish solidarity broke down completely even before the war, when it was needed in order to support the aggressive section of the Eastern European Jewry. And the most treacherous opponent of this stratum in Europe, the Czar, became an ally of the rich Jews of Western Europe, being supported by them with all the means at their disposal.

Haman, Imperial Chancellor of King Ahasuerus, was the original prototype of a pogrom-instigator, and was considered by the ancient Jews as the enemy who should be suspended from a gallows fifty feet in height. The Czar maltreated the Jewish people far more cruelly than ever Haman had done, but the capitalist Jews not only did not desire his ruin, but even supported him by means of the loans they granted him, thus repeatedly prolonging his existence. For Mordecai had become a poor tailor, and Esther had not risen to the dignity of a queen, but had been dragged off to an Argentine bordello.

ARE THE JEWS A RACE?

It is precisely at the time when the theory of the pure race is set up and the Jews are raised to the dignity of being the model of a pure, exclusive race, that they begin to present the profoundest cleavages due to class hostilities, which here coincide with a cultural hostility. The contrast between capitalist and proletarian Jews imparts to the present migrations of the Jews an entirely different character, as well as entirely different effects, than formerly. Kaplun-Kogan has excellently characterised the difference in the nature of these migrations, but he has made the rather poor inference that the difference is based on their having been formerly bearers of economic progress, while now they are bearers of economic retrogression.[17]

"Economic progress" means the progress of capitalism, and for this there are needed not only means of production but also proletarians. The means of production do not become capital until they begin to be applied by the proletarians. American capitalism could not have made its enormous advances within the last few decades if it had not been for the immense influx of proletarian masses from Europe. All the proletarians who set forth from an environment of economic obstruction to an environment favorable to progress, and who, in the latter environment, place themselves at the disposal of their employers, thus became an element of economic progress. At first, they are an unconscious influence in this direction, but later they become its conscious agents, for their migration has made

[17] Kaplun-Kogan, *op cit.*, pp. 58, 147.

178

them more capable of struggle. And in spite of their inevitable great illiteracy as a result of the Czarist barbarism, they were far superior in mental swiftness and in theoretical ability in the United States, as a city population, to other immigrants who came from the most backward agricultural districts.

The Jewish workers' movement in the United States is one of the most active pioneers of social progress.

CHAPTER IX

ZIONISM BEFORE THE WAR

THE immense transformation in the conditions of Russia has not been without its effect on Jewish thought, and it has awakened to life the most varied aspirations among the Russian Jews, many forms of the ambition to defend themselves against their enemies, and to emerge from their desperate situation.

In so far as these ambitions are not limited to a mere running away, to mere emigration, they consist in the effort to increase the strength of Judaism by means of solidarity: either through *proletarian* solidarity, by a union of the Jewish proletarians with the non-Jewish proletarians, or by means of a general *Jewish* solidarity, by uniting the powers of the Jews of all countries with those of the Russian Jews.

The efforts to make the Jewish proletariat a part of the class struggle of the entire Russian proletariat found their feasible expression in the Jewish Workers Union (*Arbeiterbund*). Jewish socialists, proletarians as well as intellectuals, played a prominent part in both the Russian revolutions, that of 1905 as well as that of 1917. We shall merely mention this fact in passing, for a complete exposition of the circumstances would amount to writing a history of the Russian Revolution.

ZIONISM BEFORE THE WAR

The culmination of the second tendency mentioned above is *Zionism.*

After the first Russian Revolution (1905), a new tendency set in, aiming at a union of Zionism and socialism. We need not discuss this movement here, for our general consideration of Zionism will also pay some attention to its socialist phase.

The literary origin of Zionism is in Western Europe, but the real *need* of Zionism is felt only by the Jews of Eastern Europe.

The proletarian class struggle, with its socialist leadership, finds the wage workers of modern large-scale industry most accessible to its needs, and precisely this group of workers is not strongly represented among the Jewish proletarians, who furnish a larger contingent to the workers in backward forms of industry, working as individual masters, as domestic workers; the Jewish immigrants in England and America are engaged chiefly in work done at their own homes.[1] In addition, there are numerous petty traders and forms of life living from hand to mouth, on whatever resources may come to hand, *Luftmenschen,* as Max Nordau calls them, persons living on the edge of the *Lumpenproletariat.* All these elements—other things being equal—are more difficult to organise and cannot so easily be drawn into the struggle as the workers in large-

[1] With the gradual abandonment of the sweatshop system in New York, in favour of comparatively large factory centres, this condition may now be regarded as a thing of the past.—TRANSLATOR.

181

scale industry, who have been already united and schooled in team action by the mechanical process. Furthermore, the revolutionary movement had first brought about persecutions of the Jews by reactionary forces in many parts of Eastern Europe. The Jewish intelligentsia always played a prominent part among the Russian revolutionary intelligentsia; this Jewish intelligentsia therefore drew the fire of the anti-Semitic reaction and because of it the entire Jewish community was held responsible, as a race rebellious by nature. For this reason the political motives of the counter-revolution associated themselves with its economic motives to increase the already considerable sufferings of the Jews.

As a result of all these circumstances, the slogan of solidarity between the proletarians of all nations and faiths became a guiding principle only for a portion of the Jewish proletarians. For the slogan of *proletarian* solidarity the other sections of the Jewish proletariat substituted the slogan of a *national* solidarity of Judaism.

Those who became tired of the struggle or felt themselves incapable of fighting, but yet had still sufficient energy to desire not to be eliminated entirely, sought foreign shores. But were they likely to find an improvement in their situation by going abroad? Wherever the Jew—we mean the Eastern European Jew, still far from assimilation—may come, he is regarded as a foreigner among foreigners. He is nowhere certain even to be tolerated. The reactionary American workers, who keep out the Chinese and Japanese, who keep Negro workers out of their organisations, are equally opposed to Jewish immigration. The beginnings of such an attitude are already apparent. The Jew is secure against oppression only in a state in which he lives not as a foreigner, in a state—therefore—of his own nationality. Only in a real Jewish state will the emancipation of Judaism be possible.

This is the guiding thought of Zionism. Even among the circles of Western European Judaism, this idea has in recent years been replacing the idea of assimilation, of equality of rights within the existing states, which had until recently been dominant among the Jews. Zionism is coming more and more in conflict with this thought, for as assimilation progresses, the national Jewry loses in strength. It is therefore necessary to segregate Jews as sharply as possible from non-Jews.

Zionism meets anti-Semitism halfway in this effort, as well as in the fact that its goal is the removal of all Jews from the existing states.

The agreement between Zionism and anti-Semitism on these points is so strong, that there have even been Zionists who expected much gracious assistance in the realisation of their objects from the head of the Orthodox Russian nation, from the fountain-head of anti-Semitism all over the world, from the Czar of Russia.

There is no doubt of the needs that serve as the basis of the Zionist aspirations; in these needs lies their strength. But the needs may only serve as an explanation of the aspirations; it may not assure their success, which depends on entirely different factors.

In the civilised world all regions have been preempted; there is no more room for a Jewish state. It is only outside of the limits of the civilised world, and only under the tutelage and patronage of a non-Jewish national state that a Jewish community is still conceivable. For a time it was hoped to found a colony in East Africa under English suzerainty, but finally thoughts have always converged on Palestine as the indicated home for a Jewish community.

But, curiously enough, there had already been a Jewish state in Palestine, founded by Jews in exile, under the protection of a non-Jewish state; and even at that remote period—two thousand years ago—this state had not served as a very powerful attraction for the Jews living in the Diaspora. Most of the Jews chose to remain in Babylon, Damascus, Alexandria, Rome, and in other places of domicile, only a portion of them settling in Jerusalem. Most of them contented themselves with an occasional pilgrimage to the Holy City. They found that they prospered better when living as strangers among strangers than in the national state.

Nothing has since been changed in this condition. To be sure, the situation of the Polish, Hungarian and Rumanian Jews is desperate, unendurable. But the question is not whether they could live better in Palestine than now in Western Europe, but whether the founding of a Jewish community in Palestine would afford them better opportunities than revolution in their own country. In fact, it is very questionable whether all the Jews now living—though but painfully—in Eastern Europe, could find any opportunities for their existence in Palestine at all.

One of the conditions for the independent existence of a state is that it shall include all the classes necessary for its process of production under the present conditions of division of labour. This process is based on a constant exchange between city and country; a state is impossible without agriculture. But whence is the agriculture of the new Zion to be derived?

It is, of course, absurd to maintain that the Jewish race is incapable by nature of engaging in agriculture. In the days when it was far more possible to speak of the existence of a Jewish race than now, namely, in the period preceding the Babylonian Exile, the Jews were predominantly agriculturists, as were all the peoples of antiquity. Even in our day efforts to make peasants of Jews have occasionally met with success. If such efforts have never been extended and followed up, this condition is due not to the fact that the Jews are Jews, but to the fact that they are city-dwellers. While the path from country to city is easy to follow, it is difficult to retrace one's steps if they are to lead to hard manual toil and not to mere enthusiasm for nature and sport. Let anyone point out any large body of "Indo-Germanic" city-dwellers flocking to the country in order to earn their living as peasants or farm hands! Needless to say, there are none. In present-day society, earning one's living in the country is associated with conditions that are intolerable for the city dweller. There is no doubt that we are emphatically in need of a stemming of the present tide from country to city, both for hygienic as well as for economic reasons, but the conditions for such a reversal of the process may be found only in a socialist society. Even Herzl recognised this situation when he said: "Anyone who would make agriculturists out of Jews is a victim of a most peculiar delusion." [2]

Herzl indeed recognised the necessity of agriculture for the Jewish State, but in order to find a possibility for Jewish agriculture he was obliged to build up an entire Utopia.

We are well aware, however, that the replacement of the present mode of production by a higher mode of production can only emanate from centres in which capitalism has already been developed to the highest point. We are no longer living in times when men sought to establish socialist colonies in the wilderness. Industrial capitalism is the *sine qua non* of socialism. Whether it be desired to establish the Jewish state on a capitalist or on a socialist basis, the capitalist structure of society will be the necessary point of departure and it is here that we encounter a second obstacle.

How will it be possible for a powerful industry to develop in Palestine? There is no large domestic market. The rising industry would be obliged to work for the export trade

[2] *Der Judenstaat*, Leipzig, 1896, p. 23.

from the very beginning. But even in the competitive struggle on the world market, an industry—other things being equal—can maintain itself far better if it has at its disposal an extensive internal market capable of absorbing large quantities, and furnishing the basis for the industry's demand. If an industry is to become capable of meeting competition on the foreign market, without possessing a market at home, exceptionally favourable circumstances must be on its side. In Palestine, on the contrary, the conditions for the growth of industry have been as un-favourable as possible: the soil has thus far revealed no deposits of coal or of raw materials; neither ores, nor tex-tile substances, nor wood; it grows but few foodstuffs, with the result that prices of foodstuffs rise at once when im-migration increases; there are no transportation routes, no navigable rivers, no good ports, no highways; and, before the war, there was no railroad line of importance.

The conditions in Turkey had not turned out to be very favourable for an industrial boom, and these conditions were nowhere so wretched as in Palestine. No industry can be founded on Biblical reminiscences; and Palestine has hitherto produced nothing in the way of other products. Capital, in its hunt for profits—Jewish capital as well as other capital—has therefore always avoided the "Holy Land" in spite of the eager rapacity with which it has penetrated into all other countries affording any prospect of gain.

The Zionist state of the future in Palestine had therefore

not succeeded before the war in making any notable advance. According to Ruppin, 2,000,000 Jews emigrated from 1881 to 1908 from Russia, Austria and Rumania, of whom 1,600,000 went to America, almost 300,000 to Western Europe, and only 26,000 to Palestine!

We have already mentioned Nawratzki's work on the colonisation of Palestine, which is a painstaking and detailed book and which was evidently written as a labour of love. But the critical reader will not be able to form the optimistic expectations which the author draws from his material.

Immense sums have been spent by Jewish philanthropists in order to further the colonisation of Palestine. "In the foundation of the Rothschild colonies very large sums have been invested by these philanthropists alone; the amount is estimated at about fifty million francs." [3]

The Jewish Colonisation Association was given a capital of 160,000,000 marks by Baron Hirsch,[4] most of which went to the work of advancing the colonisation of Palestine. In addition, there was an uninterrupted flow of money to Palestine from many other collections and donations.

"An approximate estimate of all the moneys flowing annually into Palestine for the above-mentioned purposes would reach the figure of at least 10,000,000 francs." [5]

What has been accomplished in Palestine in the three

[3] Nawratzki, p. 495.
[4] Nawratzki, p. 100.
[5] Nawratzki, p. 109.

decades of colonising activity preceding the war, with these enormous money resources? One of the tasks was the founding of a Jewish agricultural community. "At the end of the year 1912, and including the settlements of the recently arrived Yemenites and the farm workers in the colonies and land groups, there was a country population of about 10,000." [6] As compared with the total Jewish emigration to foreign countries, this is a mere drop in the bucket.

The experiences gathered in the attempts at colonisation led to the following inference: "The costs of a farm 'are comparatively high and may fluctuate between 12,000 and 18,000 francs per family. The necessary requirements to be met by a family of colonists are *a sufficient knowledge of farming* and *enough money to pay* for one-eighth or one-fourth of the cost of the farm and, in addition, to have enough operating capital left over for the first year's operations'." [7]

Where such wealthy and experienced Jewish peasants are to come from we are not told. And, therefore, this proposition is not one that could lead to the emancipation of the Jewish proletarians in Russia.

But of course, there were also large-scale Jewish agricultural establishments which flourished. The Jewish capitalist farmers had found a difficulty, however, in the employment of Jewish proletarians from Russia as farm

[6] Nawratzki, p. 349.
[7] Nawratzki, p. 360.

hands: these Russian Jews are more exacting and less easily managed than the Arabs, for which reason the Jewish patriots have substituted Arab workers for their Jewish workers, as German patriots have frequently substituted Italian and Polish workers for their German workers. Since this device, however, conflicts with the purposes of Jewish colonisation, and since it is necessary, nevertheless, to exploit Jews as farm hands, recourse was had to the introduction of Jews from Yemen (Arabia). These Jews are at as low a cultural level as the Arabs among whom they live, are completely cut off from their European co-religionists, and have not the slightest connection with the problems of the European Jewry; but they are willing and cheap and therefore afford a possibility of solving the question of the Jewish colonisation of Palestine. "Within the last ten years, about 6,000 Yemenites have probably emigrated to Palestine." [8]

No doubt this was very fortunate for the purposes of the capitalist Jewish colonist, but it threatened to bring on a bankruptcy of the policy of inducing the Jewish proletarians of Russia to take up agriculture in Palestine.

Now for the non-agricultural Jewish population in Palestine. This population, on the whole, seems hitherto to have lived in wretched conditions, in many cases resorting to actual mendicancy. This mendicancy was not a form of street-begging, but a drawing of alms from charitable institutions supported by Jews in all countries. Nor was

[8] Nawratzki, p. 441.

it possible for the non-agricultural population to live in any other way: "Industry has as yet attained no importance in Palestine." [9]

The wages that were paid before the war may be inferred from the fact that Jewish farm hands who asked from 1.15 to 2 francs per day were considered too expensive; Arabs could be had for 1.10 francs. Efforts were made to introduce a lace industry: "A fairly good factory girl gets *as much as* 1 franc per day!" Furthermore, foodstuffs were high. The workers in the colony of Rechoboth had to pay about 45 francs per month for food alone in the years 1907 to 1910.

It should give rise to no surprise to find that the immigration to Palestine was not large and that a large percentage of this immigration consisted of aged persons who did not go to Palestine in order to work, but in order to live on charity, or on their own incomes, and to end their days in the land of their fathers. Most of the younger immigrants again set forth to other parts. Of the 1,979 Jewish emigrants leaving Odessa for Palestine in 1910, 606, or 30 per cent., were over 50 years of age. Data gathered in Jaffa show that in 1912 there arrived in that port, in addition to 350 Yemenites and 950 Bukhara Jews, 2,280 Jews from Eastern Europe (*Ashkenazim*), of whom only 30 per cent. were under the age of thirty. [10] If we calculate the absolute figures on the basis of the per-

[9] Nawratzki, p. 403.
[10] Nawratzki, p. 444.

191

centages communicated by Nawratzki—who does not furnish us with the absolute figures—we find that 684 young Jews entered Jaffa in 1912, while 790 emigrated in the same year.

In other words, there were more *young* Jews emigrating than immigrating. In spite of Sombart's "theory of the wilderness", the Jew, like any other modern man, is attracted to the large city and not to the wilderness, when in search of a livelihood.

CHAPTER X

ZIONISM AFTER THE WAR

SINCE then we have had the World War, which has by no means improved the *economic* conditions for the flourishing of a Jewish community in Palestine. To be sure, the political conditions for Jewish emigration to that region have apparently been improved, while the consequences of the war have at the same time strengthened anti-Semitism in Eastern Europe and thus increased the desire for a secure homeland for the Jewish race.

In Western Europe and America as well as in the Central Powers, the Jewish population had become exceedingly patriotic for the most part; far from standing above the warring factions, as an exclusive race or nation might have done, they plunged into the war with the greatest enthusiasm. The German Jews felt that they were only German, the French Jews that they were only French. They hated each other with all the fury of the war psychosis, and did not consider that they had any interests in common.

Neither of the two belligerent groups had the upper hand from the outset. Each was obliged to utilise every resource at its disposal. On both sides of the trenches, each government sought to obtain the full support of its proletarians, and also of its Jews. The cheapest concession that could be made to the latter was in the form of promises to support Zionism. For these promises were all to be realised at the expense of Turkey. The Central Powers, as well as the Entente, permitted the Jews to believe that their victory would result in a Jewish homeland in Palestine.

Therefore the war stimulated not only the English, French, German or other nationalism of the Jewish population, but also its specifically Jewish nationalism: Zionism. Now that the war is over, it appears that this aspiration is to be realised through the victors. The victors, in the Peace Treaty with Turkey, assigned control over Palestine to the League of Nations. In the name of the League, Palestine is to be administered by England, which will encourage the establishment of a Jewish homeland in Palestine. Of course, this is by no means equivalent as yet to the establishment of an independent Jewish state, but it may give rise to hopes of such a state. However, this will be possible only if a steady stream of Jewish emigration turns to Palestine and there creates a flourishing community. This stream would have to be a very generous one if it should introduce any essential improvement in the lot of the Eastern European Jews. We have already seen that in the twenty-seven years between 1881 and 1908, 2,000,000 Jews emigrated from Europe, but the number of Jews in Eastern Europe nevertheless increased considerably during the same period, while their situation became worse and worse. In Russia, in 1880, there were not quite 4,000,000 Jews, while in 1914, there were 6,000,000 or 7,000,000, an increase of 2,000,000 or 3,000,000. In Austria-Hungary, in 1880, there were 1,646,000 Jews, while in 1914, there were 2,260,000, an increase of more than half a million. Of the 2,000,000 Jews who emigrated, only 26,000 had turned their steps to Palestine; this means that emigration to Palestine would have to increase phenomenally if any alleviation of the condition of the Eastern European Jews should be expected from this source.

The hopes of the Zionists in this field were much raised by a calculation made by Professor Ballod in a book entitled: *Palästina als jüdisches Ansiedlungsgebiet*,[1] which was written during the war. Ballod argues in this work against a calculation set up by the German geographer, Professor Philippson, who had maintained in an article contributed to the *Berliner Tageblatt* of February 9, 1916, which is based on the professor's intimate knowledge of the countries surrounding the Mediterranean, that the stony soil of Palestine could not support a population of more than 1,200,000 persons.

Ballod also attacks a book written by the agronomist, Jakob Öttinger, entitled *Methoden und Kapitalbedarf jüdischer Kolonisation in Palästina*,[2] who believed that he was taking a very optimistic position in assuming that about 100,000 farming families could be established in

---

[1] *Pro-Palästina, Schriften des deutschen Komitees zur Förderung der jüdischen Palästinaansiedlung, Zweites Heft.*
[2] Ballod, *Palästina*, p. 18.

Palestine, affording a livelihood to 500,000 members of these families. Ballod considers it possible to settle six million persons in Palestine—not in the Palestine of to-day, but in a Palestine to be created on a new foundation. The realisation of Ballod's proposals would raise Palestine from hitherto the most neglected corner of the earth to its most highly developed state. Ballod would establish 100,000 petty farms and 1,000 large-scale enterprises, operating with the most perfect machines, and the most effective fertilisers, and producing in accordance with the most modern methods. An immense irrigation system will transform the arid land into a paradise. Öttinger counts on an average wheat crop of 600 kilogrammes per hectare, while Ballod expects an average crop of 3,000 kilogrammes; in Germany the average crop is only 2,000 kilogrammes. In the case of cotton, Ballod hopes for crops of 600 kilogrammes per hectare, while in the United States only 200 or 250 kilogrammes are produced for the same area.

But Ballod calculates that the entire immense transformation of Palestine which would make it possible to achieve such record crops and would make the country a home for 6,000,000 persons, would cost only 5,000,000,000 gold marks, while Öttinger had calculated a year before that 2,000,000,000 francs would be necessary in order to settle half a million persons in Palestine.

It must be that Ballod expects to pay lower prices than Öttinger. For instance, Ballod says: "The erection of ordinary houses, together with wells and cisterns and the necessary irrigation plants, could be carried out for 1,000 marks." Öttinger, on the other hand, declares: "In accordance with previous experiences in Palestine, the dwelling of a worker will cost *at least* 2,000 francs; . . . connecting up the farm with an irrigation system would probably cost 500 francs more." [3]

Even Öttinger's worker's cottage, costing 2,500 francs (including irrigation system), will hardly be a palace. Later Zionists prefer, however, to take their material from Ballod. As late as 1919, Davis Triesch declares in his little book, *Palästina und die Juden, Tatsachen und Ziffern:* "For 1,000 marks, a solidly built modest house can be erected. *As a matter of fact, houses have recently been erected at this price in Germany.*" [4] Lest the reader imagine that Triesch refers to the construction of birdcages, he adds: "Houses *of five rooms* or more must be erected for 1,000 marks, depending on the mode of construction."

"Facts and figures" [5] of this kind must cause us to wonder why not only the entire Jewish race but also all of Christendom is not found flocking to this promised land, whose fabulously cheap houses have a striking way of reminding us of its fabulously large clusters of grapes,

[3] Ottinger, *Jüdische Kolonisation*, p. 67.
[4] Triesch, *op. cit.*, p. 26.
[5] *Tatsachen und Ziffern*, an allusion to the subtitle of Triesch's book. —TRANSLATOR.

each cluster of which must be carried by two men, with the aid of a pole, because of its great size.[6]

But even if all of Ballod's calculations should be correct, we are not informed as to the period within which they are to be made real. Even the far more sober Öttinger gives us no definite suggestions on this point. On page 100 of his book, Öttinger outlines a project for the foundation of new colonies:

"In accordance with this plan, in the course of about 12 years, 30 new Jewish points of support, having an initial agricultural population of 3,000 families, or 12,000 to 15,000 persons, would be established. In addition, about 30,000 Jews of other occupations would probably be attracted into the country by reason of this colonising." These colonies would require a capital of 77,500,000 gold francs. But the 45,000 new immigrants provided here are quite a different figure from Ballod's 6,000,000.

To be sure, Öttinger later adds that the colonisation of Palestine might, under favourable circumstances, proceed at a more rapid rate, in which connection he mentions the possibility of housing half a million new settlers in Palestine, but with the cautious interpolation: "Of course, this figure should be regarded as entirely hypothetical, and *the question as to the time* required for the colonisation of such

---

[6] "And they came unto the brook of Eshcol, and cut down from thence a branch with one cluster of grapes, and they bare it between two upon a staff; and they brought of the pomegranates and of the figs."—Numbers xiii, 23.

a number of colonists should for the present be entirely left out of account." [7]

Yet, this question is by no means of little account to Zionism. Whatever Zionism does not accomplish in the immediate future, it will never accomplish, as we shall see later. And it is entirely impossible to throw great masses of Jewish colonists into Palestine in the immediate future.

The war did not spare Palestine. The economic situation of the country was, like that of all other countries, far worse after the war than before it.

The situation in Palestine in the year 1919 may be inferred from a private letter which I have received from a Zionist whose name I may not divulge, but the name does not matter for the present. I have received confirmation of the contents of this letter from many quarters. The letter, which was written in Palestine and dated October 30, 1919, says among other things:

"We are no longer of our former opinion as to immigration. . . . We are coming to the conclusion that a mass immigration is not only undesirable at the present time, but that it would be an *outright cruelty,* particularly for two reasons:

"1. *Hygienic reasons.* The whole region (cities as well as the country districts) is infected with malaria, not to mention a number of other avoidable infectious diseases, such as trachoma (an inflammation of the eyes). Palestine is in need of a thorough housecleaning before it will be

[7] Öttinger, *op. cit.,* p. 104.

199

suitable for colonisation. We found many of the Jewish colonies or villages in the most wretched condition; every settler in some towns was actually either incapable of work or hopelessly run down. The same condition was found in the cities. Although Jerusalem lies above the normal mosquito line, great numbers of mosquitoes are found there. A group of heroic young Jews from Poland arrived here after incredible adventures at the beginning of this year. We found most of them ill. The local medical station of the American Zionists has accomplished much; for instance, it annihilated the mosquitoes at Safed in six weeks, by having oil poured on the water in the cisterns. As a consequence of the visit paid by Brandeis, this station will achieve even greater things. But it will be a long time before the country is healthy enough to receive a mass immigration, for the draining of the swamps will involve far more labour than the oiling of the tanks.

"2. *Employment.* Palestine is full of Jewish beggars today. The Jewish population of Jerusalem and other so-called 'holy' places have been accustomed to live on the gifts of their co-religionists abroad. These donations were cut off during the war and cannot be renewed now because of the present situation of the Jews in Eastern Europe. Much misery is the result. In Safed, the Jewish population decreased from 10,000 to 3,000. These persons were not accustomed to work, but they have now been converted to the idea and are shouting for work. New industries are urgently required, and we have carefully considered the possibility of such industries; for instance, printing, the production of articles used in synagogues, of preserved fruit, garments, etc. But you may imagine that such industries must be built on a firm foundation if sweatshops and other undesirable European (and not only European; the factories of Damascus, for example, are said to be frightful) concomitants of industry are to be avoided. . . .

"I know very well what this delay will mean for the Jews of Eastern Europe who are ready to flock into this country by the millions. Unfortunately, Palestine cannot, even under the most favourable circumstances, undertake for many years to absorb in any adequate way all those that are prepared to come. The best informed authority on matters of the colonisation of Palestine, Artur Ruppin, has calculated—in a book that appeared last April, *Der Aufbau des Landes Israel*—that 20 years will be required under favourable conditions to increase the present Jewish population to 1,000,000 or 1,250,000, and that the increase in the number of Jewish workers employed in public works cannot be made more than 15,000 per year in the near future.

"The best authorities do not doubt that the country can be made to support a numerous population after the lapse of two generations. But this is but sad consolation for the victims of pogroms in our own day. But we cannot have our cake and eat it too.

"If Palestine is to become an asylum of refuge, it cannot be a truly healthy community. If it is to be built up on sound economic foundations, the would-be fugitives will have to bide their time."

Since this letter was written, the economic conditions of the Jews in Palestine have improved considerably. Thanks to the active support of Jews all over the world, and to the energy and enthusiasm of the Jewish immigrants, much has been accomplished in the way of road construction, irrigation systems, agricultural settlements, and cultural institutions. An absolutely new Jewish city, Tel Aviv, has sprung into being, on a site that was a mere sand dune before the war; also, a Jewish university has recently been created.

The character of the Jewish immigration has changed considerably. While before the war it consisted chiefly of beggars, who lived in many parts of the world on Jewish charity, it is now workers and intellectuals at the prime of life who are coming, able and willing to reconquer the land of their fathers in the sweat of their brows, and, if need be, by superhuman exertions.

Anyone who has doubted the possibility of the Jewish people's showing energy, resolution and intelligence in this crisis, must surely have changed his mind by reason of the work of Zionist reconstruction in Palestine.

To be sure, the giving of such an object lesson can hardly have been necessary, for no one really doubts that the Jewish race possesses great capabilities. The point at issue is not whether the Jews have ability, but whether the accomplishments of the Jewish cultural work in Palestine may justify the assumption that this region may become the centre for a great emancipation of the entire Jewish people, may put an end to the condition of the Diaspora, and gather the Jews of all the world into one great national state.

Our first question should be: How long will it be possible for the Jewish rehabilitation process in Palestine to proceed at a fairly rapid rate?

In view of the extremely unfavourable natural conditions offered by Palestine in the work of creating new arable soil and maintaining the excellence of that already acquired, as well as in the work of securing routes of communication, without which agricultural colonies cannot prosper, truly superhuman powers will be required, and the exertion of such efforts will deprive the workers of every vestige of a higher standard of living.

Of the Jewish immigrants who have come hitherto, and I do not mean former peasants, or ditch-diggers, but in great measure intellectuals, many—impelled by a patriotic enthusiasm—have willingly submitted to these labours and privations without a murmur.

But enthusiasm of this type has always been the special gift of a small group of chosen persons, and even in such cases it is not a permanent acquisition. The hard toil of the daily grind usually succeeds in soon crushing all heaven-storming enthusiasms, and in the long run a new social order cannot be built up on overwork and on exertions greater than those formerly borne by the individuals in question.

The accessions of new enthusiasts must ultimately dwindle, and the ranks of those now at work will be thinned in the course of time.

Even in South America, and in present-day Russia or in the United States, where the natural conditions are far more favourable, and where political obstacles to the farming activities of the Jews are as little present as in Palestine, we have not observed that any isolated attempts to transform Jews into peasants have led—by their success—to any widespread emulation on the part of most Jews. We have no reason to assume that conditions in Palestine will be any different, once the period of the first flash of enthusiasm is past.

Already we find a predominant tendency on the part of the Jews in Palestine to settle in the cities. Tel Aviv is growing far more rapidly than are the agricultural colonies. This city is now only six years old, and already it has 40,000 inhabitants. There were 80,000 Jews in Palestine in 1921, who had increased to 120,000 by the end of 1924. In other words, the entire increase in population is accounted for by the existence of the city of Tel Aviv. In addition, there are 40,000 Jews in Jerusalem and 12,000 in Jaffa.

Reports from the cities themselves inform us that employment for artisans is increasing very slowly and that the number of vagrants (*Luftmenschen*) and intellectuals constitutes a percentage of the population that is rapidly increasing.

In other words, these cities will soon be facing the same problem that has been encountered by the Jews in the cities of Eastern Europe; in fact, the problem will be a more serious one, for the European Jews are at least living among a dense population which, though not Jewish, is nevertheless agricultural.

These difficulties will increase as the Jewish population of Palestine begins to live on its own work, ceasing to live on foreign philanthropy, as it did before the war. With the rise of a working class will come—even in Palestine— an increase in socialistic ideas, which will condition a sharp opposition of many Jewish elements to capitalism within Zionism. These contrasts became quite apparent even at the last Zionist Congress at Vienna; they will necessarily increase and express themselves with more and more definiteness.

As this condition increases, the interest shown by the Jewish capitalists of the world in Zionism will lose its ardour. But without constant accessions of new capital, the Jewish work of cultivation in Palestine will not make much progress.

As yet, there has never been much Jewish immigration. We have seen that the total increase of the number of Jews in Palestine was only 40,000 during the four-year period above mentioned; in other words, an average increase of 10,000 per year. The rate may since have risen to 20,000 or 30,000 per year. These figures are large when compared with the small area of the country, already holding *six hundred thousand* inhabitants.

But how insignificant are these figures when compared with the total growth of Judaism throughout the world! Annually this increase amounts to ten times the size of the Jewish immigration into Palestine. Under these circumstances, how could this country ever absorb more than an imperceptible fraction of the world's Jewish population?

No doubt the promised land will some day be able to offer work to more inhabitants than at present, once all the projected great irrigation plants, highways, railroads, etc., have been completed, but the volume of the immigration tending in that direction will never be so great as to reduce in any way the number of Jews living in Europe and America, and thus to solve the present Jewish question.

At best, it might bring about the following partial accomplishment: the number of Jews in Palestine may increase more rapidly than the number of non-Jews in the country (the Arabs) and the new Jewish state, although it will never embrace the great mass of the world's Jewish population, may nevertheless be predominantly Jewish in tone.

But even this prospect is not likely to be fulfilled.

To be sure, the length of time that would be required by Jewish colonisation in order to impress a Jewish stamp upon Palestine would be no argument against such colonisation, provided time were working in favour of Zionism as it has worked in favour of socialism; in other words, if the conditions for the realisation of Zionism were progressively improving in the course of the economic and political evolution. But these conditions do not apply in the case of Zionism, and this constitutes its fundamental weakness. Zionism cannot afford to wait, *for the political conditions for its realisation are rapidly becoming worse.* Whatever Zionism does not attain within the next few years, it will never attain at all.

For Zionism is not a progressive movement, but a reactionary movement. Zionism aims not at following the line of necessary evolution, but of putting a spoke in the wheel of progress.

Zionism denies the right of self-determination of nations, instead of which it proclaims the doctrine of historical rights, which is breaking down everywhere today, even where it is supported by the greatest powers.

The idea of democracy, of the self-determination of nations, is indissolubly connected with modern economic evolution, and is thus made irresistible.[8] This is not only true today for Europe, but it is beginning to be true for Asia also.

The outcome of the World War might have involved a considerable progress in international relations, if the victors had everywhere accepted the democratic doctrine and recognised throughout, as a principle, the self-determina-

[8] I have discussed this subject in detail in my book, *Die Befreiung der Nationen,* Stuttgart, 1917.

tion of nations. But they permitted themselves to be guided only by their love of power; they condescended to apply the notion of the self-determination of nations only at such points where it was convenient for them. Wherever an application of this doctrine might have strengthened their former opponents, they replaced it quite arbitrarily with other guiding notions, such as that of strategic boundaries, of monopolisation of the treasures of the soil or of traffic routes, as well as that of historical rights, the claim of a nation to the restoration of the boundaries of its state as they existed centuries ago, under entirely different circumstances.

Among the many antiquated legal claims which the little protégés of the great victors filed with the latter, the most ancient and moth-eaten is the historical claim of the Jews to Palestine. This claim is two thousand years old, and during these two thousand years the Jews have completely ceased to be a nation. They have not only lost their common territory, but even their common language. The only language that today might be considered a living Jewish language, namely, "Yiddish," is a mutilated German. A faint tinge of Jewish nationalism is attained by this language only when it is set down in writing, not when it is spoken. It is German written in Hebrew characters.

Palestine does not yet have a Jewish population of any importance as to size. The single city of New York contains fourteen times as many Jews as Palestine, where the Jewish population amounts to not more than one-eighth

of the total population, of which the great majority consists of Arabs. There are 620,000 Arabs as compared with
120,000 Jews; as economic conditions improve, the number
of Arabs will increase as well as the number of Jews.
Palestine could not very well be isolated from the neighbouring countries, which are entirely Arabic.

There is hardly any possibility that the Jews in Palestine
will become more numerous than the Arabs. But every
attempt made by the advancing Jewry in that country to
displace the Arabs cannot fail to arouse the fighting spirit
of the latter, in which opposition to the Jews the Arabs
of Palestine will be more and more assured of the support
of the entire Arab population of Asia Minor, in whose
eyes the Jews appear as foreign rulers or as allies of the
English oppressor.

It is a delusion to imagine that the Jews arriving from
Europe and America will ever succeed in convincing the
Arabs that Jewish rule in this country will ever redound to
the advantage of the Arabs themselves.

In the early days of Zionism, people were blind to this
difficulty. Little more attention was paid to the Arabs
than was paid to the Indians in North America. Only
occasionally is it remembered that Palestine is already an
occupied country. It is then simply assumed that its
former inhabitants will be pushed aside in order to make
room for the incoming Jews. Ballod, for instance, dis-
cusses as follows the question of what is to be done in the
way of claiming all of Palestine for Jewish colonisation:

"In the case of a mass colonisation, mere individual purchases of land from the Arab proprietors of large holdings would not be sufficient; on the other hand, in order that real-estate prices may not rise to fabulous heights, a Jewish chartered company must be given the right to expropriate land in return for adequate compensation." [9] Ballod also says that the petty peasants, the fellahs, will not provide much trouble. In his opinion, they would "gladly leave Palestine if they should be offered opportunities elsewhere, for instance in Northern Syria or Babylonia, if the latter is to be reawakened to life by large-scale engineering operations, to obtain better conditions". But who is to offer them these "better conditions"?

Ballod, himself, therefore expects that there will be trouble between Jews and Arabs in Palestine. His book was written at a time when Ballod was convinced of the victory of the Central Powers. We therefore find him expressing, in a special chapter entitled "The Central Powers and Zionism", the advantages offered by Zionism to the Central Powers. He points out "that it is to the interest of Germany and Austria to have large masses of Jews settled in Turkey",[10] in the first place, because this would mean an accession of population to their ally, Turkey, which would by that time have been somewhat denuded of population and resources, and in the second place, because the Eastern European Jews who would furnish this immigration would speak German and would thus help

[9] Ballod, *Palästina*, p. 30.   [10] Ballod, *op. cit.*, p. 27.

advance Turkey's trade with the Central Powers, and, finally, for the reason that the Jews in Palestine would furnish a counterweight to the Arabs, who favoured England.

But the fact now is that England has won the war, and the Arabs have become as burdensome to England as they once were to the Turks. The Zionists now present the reverse side of the medal and extol the Jewish colonists in Palestine as England's allies against the Arab aspirations for independence.

In spite of all these changes, one condition remains permanent: the dependence of Jewish colonisation on the victorious European great powers, and the opposition of the colonists to the Arabs. Both are necessary results of the given economic and political conditions, and each of the two factors gives strength to the other in rapid alternation. Here we find the profoundest cause for the untenability of Zionism. Jewish colonisation in Palestine must collapse as soon as the Anglo-French hegemony over Asia Minor (including Egypt) collapses, and this is merely a question of time, perhaps of the very near future.

The war immensely strengthened the nationalism of the Arabs. The English themselves aided considerably in this process by appealing to the Arabs as allies against the Turkish régime. Now they cannot exorcise the powers which they thus have conjured.[11] The spirit of national

[11] "Die ich rief, die Geister,
    Werd' ich nun nicht los."
                —Goethe, *Der Zauberlehrling*, 1797.

self-determination is irresistible in Western Asia as everywhere today, once it has seized the masses of the people, and such is the case now with the Arabs. Arabia is now practically independent. Mesopotamia, Egypt, Syria, will become independent in the course of a few decades, and they will more and more deprive the European protectorate, which they must accept for the present, of all real authority.

There is no longer any doubt of the final victory of the Arabian people; the question merely is whether this victory is to be obtained by the peaceful method of a successive forcing of concessions, or by a period of wild guerilla warfare and bloody insurrections. The English mode of government points rather to the former, the French rather to the latter methods. In whatever way the process of transformation may be realised, the poor, weak Jewish settlers in Palestine will be the chief sufferers, during the battle of the Arabs for independence, as well as after their victory. Of all the European elements in Asia Minor, the Jews will be least able to defend themselves, as well as least capable of escape, and yet they will be treated as the worst enemies, because their colonising the country will prove that they intend to remain in it and not only make the former inhabitants dependent on them but even drive them out entirely.

Thus it may be considered truly fortunate for the Jews, who would be the sufferers, that the Zionist colonisation policy will very probably have great difficulty in getting started. We may therefore hope that the number of victims to the policy of Zionism will not be very great; this policy aims at bottom at nothing else than to transplant—at immense cost and with the greatest sacrifices of those concerned—enthusiastic Jews from regions in which anti-Jewish pogroms are subsiding, into a country where such pogroms are likely to ensue on a larger scale, if the Zionist programme should be successful to any extent that is at all perceptible.

This distortion of the original intentions into their precise opposite is inevitable whenever men base their conduct in the present time not on an investigation of the present, but on a submission to phantoms conjured up from a hoary antiquity.

But the dangers to the Jews who are lured to Palestine by a Messianic aspiration do not exhaust all the baleful effects of Zionism. It is perhaps far worse that Zionism means a wasting of the fortunes and resources of the Jews in a wrong direction, at a moment when their true destinies are being decided on an entirely different arena, for which decision it would be necessary for them to concentrate all their forces.

It is not in Palestine, but in Eastern Europe, that the destinies of the suffering and oppressed portion of Jewry are being fought out. Not for a few thousand Jews, or at most a few hundred thousand, but for a population of between eight and ten million. Emigration abroad cannot help them, no matter whither it may be turned. Their destiny is intimately connected with that of the *revolution,* in *their own country.*

The methods of the Bolsheviks are not those of the Western European Social-Democracy. The Bolsheviks will not be able to found a modern socialist state. What they are really establishing is a bourgeois revolution, which will assume forms corresponding to the social condition of present-day Russia, resembling in many ways the forms of the great French Revolution toward the end of the Eighteenth Century. Among its other effects, the French Revolution liberated the Jews in France, giving them full rights of citizenship. The same accomplishment will be included among the permanent achievements of the Russian Revolution for all of Eastern Europe, unless the Revolution succumbs to the most savage counter-revolution. But the struggle in Eastern Europe now is not only a struggle for political freedom and for the rights of the Jews to change their domicile. The conditions are also being prepared for an enhancement of their economic situation. In addition to the emancipation of the Jews, the emancipation of the peasants also will be one of the achievements of the revolution in Eastern Europe. A more prosperous peasantry will take the place of the present impoverished peasantry, thus creating a greater internal market for urban industry. Once peace has been reestablished in Eastern Europe, industry, and with it transportation, will necessarily develop with giant strides; the urban population will find abundant employment and food, and the great

214

mass of the Jewish population will find it possible to rise from conditions of life in which they have hardly emerged from the *lumpenproletariat,* to the conditions of the proletariat in large-scale industry, as a portion of which class they may then take part in the upward struggle of the entire class.

Herein only is there a possibility for the Jewish masses to achieve a truly human status. Zionism cannot strengthen them in this effort. Zionism will weaken them at the historically decisive moment by promulgating an ambition which amounts practically to a desertion of the colours.

CHAPTER XI

PURE RACES AND MIXED RACES

WE cannot take leave of Zionism before discussing another one of its arguments, its last argument, which will lead us back to the question of race.

It may appear to be a paradox, but it is a fact, that not a few Jews look with some misgiving on the emancipation of the Jews in Eastern Europe. They understand, and rightly so, that this emancipation will extend into the east of Europe the assimilation of the Jews that has been going on in the west for some time. For when the artificial exclusiveness of the Jews is terminated, when the ghetto ceases to exist, their assimilation will become everywhere inevitable.

Only in those regions of Eastern Europe in which the Jews were settled together in great numbers and artificially cut off from their environment, have they been able to preserve their national peculiarities. With the emancipation of the Jews in Eastern Europe, the last reservoir still feeding the Jewish community of the whole world will disappear, the last obstacle to its gradual assimilation. Judaism will then cease to exist as a separate body.

To be sure, this process will take place under circumstances which lift all the Jews still oppressed out of the

216

slough in which they may still be living, into the full status of human beings. But Jewish nationalism regards the conservation of traditional *Judaism* as more important than the elevation of the Jewish *individual*.

Jews who regard the matter thus are in many cases quite progressive in their other views. As is so often the case in modern society, where it is found necessary to render conservative and radical thought compatible, the race theory plays a prominent part here also.

It is declared to be urgently necessary to erect Palestine into a world ghetto, in which a great number of Jews are to be confined and cut off from the surrounding world, because in this way only can the Jewish race be protected against admixture and preserved as a race.

For the Jews are a pure race, and it is only the pure races that are called upon to achieve the highest performances. Race mixture degrades human types and lowers their cultural capacity. In other words, we should be impelled to believe that the cultural capacity of mankind decreases with its increase in culture, for an increase in culture is synonymous with an increase in international communications and contacts, and therefore in race mixtures also.

One of the most prominent advocates of the Palestinian world ghetto as a means of preserving the race purity of the Jews is Zollschan. Sharp and correct though his criticisms even of Chamberlain may be, he nevertheless exploits without question the most untenable of Chamberlain's

217

theories, namely, the theory that exalted human qualities may be found only in the pure races. Zollschan says:

"Chamberlain's book, *The Foundations of the Nineteenth Century*, has been attacked with a vehemence that has been directed to but few other works; and in most cases these attacks were well founded. But the turning point, the nucleus of Chamberlain's system, namely, his emphasis of the ennobling effects of race purity and of the destructive results of race chaos, is *unquestionably* sound. . . . Chamberlain properly observes that the normal course of development is not from race to racelessness, but from a politically conditioned racelessness to a *sharper and sharper definition of race, the quintessence of the race being expressed in the genius, the hero.* . . .

"Chamberlain says he cares very little for anthropological subdivisions; 'by *race* I mean that emphasis of specific essential characteristics and of the universal power of performance; that exaltation of the entire being, which is attained under very specific conditions of selection, mingling, in-breeding—but only under these very specific conditions, in which case it results, however, invariably; in other words, with the certainty of a natural law. . . .'

"In the case of the bastard, the individual abilities may increase, while the general, 'instinctive' abilities (characteristics) disappear; precisely the latter constitute the potential factor giving rise to all real greatness.

"In the case of crossing between members of widely separate races, the constitutional type is lost in their posterity, although the latter may quite frequently be well equipped as far as individual aptitudes are concerned. . . .

"*Doubtless* the force of heredity is far more significant in the case of the pure races. It is certain that in favourably bastardised races the kinetic cultural energy will constantly prevail, while in the pure inbred races the potential cultural energy will always prevail; but that only the latter is the fruitful soil from which the ingenious power of creation as well as the artistic and moral genius may grow forth.

"This distinction between inbred and mongrel races makes clear to us the value of race purity." [1]

It is only with ill-concealed astonishment that we can receive this anti-Semitic-Zionist-bastardisation of Chamberlain's pure race vagaries at the hands of Zollschan— otherwise an intelligent man. The race, defining itself with increasing sharpness, and whose quintessence is the genius, the hero, the race which represents nothing short of an exaltation of the entire being, in which the potential cultural energy will always be predominant—this is in truth a "race chaos" which is based on nothing but the energetic use of the words "doubtless", "without doubt", "with certainty", which are applied the more emphatically, the less definite the conceptions associated with them.

The most amusing point about the whole matter is the fact that Zollschan, at the beginning of his book, himself rejects the "nobility of race of the modern Teutons as

[1] *Das Rassenproblem,* pp. 264-270.

advanced by Gobineau, Richard Wagner, and Houston Stewart Chamberlain",[2] and with reason, for:

"Chamberlain ascertained that the Jews owe their origin to the crossing of three races entirely different from each other: the Semites, the Hittites, the Amorites. . . . The crossing between the Semites, Hittites and Amorites, is designated by Chamberlain as outright 'incest'; in the destinies of the Jewish nation resulting from this mingling, as well as in its mental unfruitfulness, Chamberlain beholds an *inevitable fate* which necessarily intervened with the certainty of a natural law, and from which the race will never be able to escape." [3]

Yet this same Chamberlain is accepted as a cast-iron basis by the Zionist race theoreticians!

This seems absurd; yet it is quite simple; Zollschan has only to prove that the Jews give evidence of great mental achievement, of much genius, such as only a pure race can develop, according to Chamberlain. It will follow as a self-evident consequence that they must be a pure race, and it would be equivalent to committing a sin against the holy spirit of history, if one should sully their purity with a mingling with other races, by bastardising them! Therefore the Zionist world-ghetto becomes the necessary goal for all Jews!

Unfortunately, this subtle reasoning is not a sufficient refutation of the fact that the Jews are a mixed race—and

[2] Zollschan, *op. cit.*, p. 32.
[3] Zollschan, *ibid.*, pp. 152, 153.

not the Jews alone, for every cultural race is a mixed race. If only "pure races" are the native soil from which the "ingenious power of creation and artistic and moral genius may grow forth", if the bastard races show no such qualities, we shall probably have to retrace our steps almost to the purity of the ape-man before we encounter the last remnants of these "generic" capacities. In the case of the cultural races, they must have long since expired, for the "bastardisation" of these races is true "beyond a doubt".

The view is no doubt very widespread that "mixed races for the most part emphasise only the defects and vices of their progenitors, not their favourable points", and Zoll-schan presents this view as "established today".[4] But, as a matter of fact, this principle is as little accepted as the other "undoubted" truths on which Zollschan bases his argument in this case.

We have already seen that the concept of the "pure" race is borrowed from the realm of domestic animals. It loses its point altogether when applied to the varieties, to the geographical races of wild animals, and even to the races of humans, in so far as they are geographical in character. All the learning of our race theoreticians and the "sharpened glance of our day for that which is in the blood" are based in the last analysis merely on a constant confusion of the most varied conceptions of race. To Chamberlain's honour be it said that he makes this idiocy quite clear to us. Again and again he places the experi-

[4] Zollschan, *ibid.*, p. 264.

ences of history on a par with the experiences gathered in artificial selection:

"The history of our own race teaches us with an eloquent tongue what we are also taught by every race horse, every pure-bred fox terrier, every Cochin-China hen!" [5]

Chamberlain alleges that the Hellenic people are an example of this process.

In an earlier passage,[6] Chamberlain observes that perhaps no "other question encounters such black ignorance even among highly educated, even learned, men, as the question concerning the essence and significance of the conception of 'race'". Chamberlain then turns against Virchow, who had demanded equality before the law for the various races and had advocated a cult of personality as opposed to the cult of race.

"As if the whole course of history did not prove to us the close connection between personality and race, the conditioning of the nature of personality by the nature of its race, and the connection of the power of personality with certain conditions of its blood! And as if the scientific breeding of plants and animals did not afford us an immensely varied and reliable material, with the aid of which we may learn both the conditions as well as the significance of 'race'. Do the (rightly) so-called 'noble' races of animals, the Limousin draught-horses, the American trotters, the Irish race-horses, the absolutely dependable hunting

[5] *Foundations of the Nineteenth Century,* vol. i, p. 272. German edition: *Die Grundlagen des XIX. Jahrhunderts.*

[6] Chamberlain, *op. cit.,* p. 264 *et seq.*

dogs—do these arise by accident and promiscuity? Are
they the result of granting the animals equality before the
law, of feeding them all on the same fodder and subjecting
them all to the same rod? No, they arise by sexual (*sic!*)
selection and by strict preservation of the purity of the
race. . . . A continuous condition of promiscuity between
two prominent animal races will invariably lead to a destruction of the most outstanding characteristics of both.
Why should mankind be an exception?"

This question can embarrass only such persons whose
"black ignorance" is so great as to prevent them from
distinguishing between the races of domestic animals and
other races, and who may believe that the laws of the
stud-farm are the universal laws of nature and of human
history, persons who imagine that the "race" of the Hel-
lenes and the race of Cochin-China hens were produced in
exactly the same way.

In the case of the latter, there is no doubt that "a permanent condition of promiscuity" with another race will
"degrade" both races. The organism of the domestic animal is not an end in itself, but a means to an end. Its
efficiency and excellence are not estimated by its power of
performance to the advantage of its own preservation and
procreation, but by its utility for the specific human purpose for which the animal has been bred. Its efficiency in
this connection will increase with its specialization, with the
increasing one-sidedness of specific organs. This one-
sidedness is decreased by crossing a highly bred race with

another race, presenting peculiarities of an entirely different type. In this way the special value inherent in each of the two races from the standpoint of the purposes of man, may easily be decreased, and the pure race—to this extent—"degraded".

But in the case of animals who are not domestic animals, efficiency must be measured by a different standard. The standard now becomes, not their efficiency in subserving the purposes of others, but their efficiency in answering the requirements of the preservation of their own organism and its own posterity. In the case of pure races, in other words, such races whose efficiency for a certain end proposed by man has been enhanced by a one-sided development, the efficiency for the purposes of their own organism may indeed increase by crossing the race with another and thus reducing its one-sided qualities.

As a matter of fact, breeders rather frequently resort to a crossing of pure races, either in order to attain new race characteristics, or in order to infuse increased energy and power of resistance into an over-refined, enervated race, by means of crossing.

Even Chamberlain admits the possibility of improving the race in this manner, by crossing. But "only very specific and limited blood-minglings are favourable to an ennobling of a race or to the establishment of a new race Here again the clearest and most unambiguous evidence is furnished by the breeding of animals. The blood-mingling must be for a limited time only, it must furthermore b adapted to the purpose; not all minglings, but only certain minglings may serve as a basis for race improvement. In limiting the time, I mean that the supply of new blood must be introduced very swiftly, after which it must cease at once." [7]

Continuous blood-mingling is tantamount to a "baleful, destructive condition, *a sin against nature*", nature meaning—in Chamberlain's eyes—fox-terriers and Cochin-China hens. But in the natural state there is no breeder to choose the breeding couples and to regulate the supply of new blood in such manner as to limit it to a swift introduction, after which the supply is cut off. Nor is man today—as yet—bred artificially. Humans never mated under Chamberlain's conditions.

To be sure, man resembles the domestic animals in his tendency to a one-sided development owing to the division of labor and to specialisation. This one-sidedness is easily overcome in cases where callings vary from generation to generation. But such one-sidedness may be developed to a high point where occupations are hereditary. This condition will be naturally attained in cases where the one-sidedness of the vocation is not an adaptation to social peculiarities, but to peculiarities of nature, to a specific natural environment, resulting in a specific mode of production. Particularly the mental characteristics (the nervous system), which are of course more variable and more capable of accommodation than the somatic elements

[7] Chamberlain, *op. cit.*, p. 284.

(skeleton, muscles, etc.), may here attain the most extreme forms; a race of horsemen may develop into a state of bloodthirsty savagery; a race of farmers into a condition of cowardly enervation; isolated in the mists of a lonely mountain range, a race may develop a gloomy and fretful mysticism, while an active condition of social contact may produce—under a cloudless sky—the most frivolous and arrogant joy of life. A mingling of such elements may, under such circumstances, produce very desirable consequences.

But such minglings may particularly be of great advantage in cases where a continuous process of in-breeding has imparted a pathological character to certain one-sided peculiarities. There is hardly any doubt that in-breeding will not be injurious under all circumstances. But it has been recognised that in-breeding leads to swift degeneration where pathological predispositions are involved. Even Zollschan admits this, although he is quite enthusiastically in favour of in-breeding:

"In-breeding—unless certain vicious conditions such as tuberculosis, lues, alcoholism, psychoses, have gained a foothold in a family—is by no means so pernicious as is generally assumed, even in the case of very close alliances within the same family. If constitutional pathogenic germs are present, these will, to be sure, attain enormous proportions; but healthy constitutions are by no means ruined in this process." [8]

[8] *Das Rassenproblem,* p. 266.

PURE RACES AND MIXED RACES

The more civilisation develops, the more artificial and unnatural becomes the environment in which the majority live. The number of persons obliged to live in cities, to work indoors, increases; the nervous system is forced to develop along narrower and narrower channels. These conditions make the organism far more receptive to germs of disease. At the same time, an extending of the artificial environment tends to limit the effects of the struggle for existence with surrounding nature, to prolong the life of diseased organisms, to render propagation possible to such organisms. Under these circumstances, in-breeding must be particularly injurious, and a mingling of varied elements must be of exceptional advantage. The increasing mingling of races by reason of the increase in world traffic may probably be considered as one of the most powerful factors opposing the tendency to a debasing of "race" by civilisation. The more we turn our backs on nature, the more necessary becomes a mingling of races.

Our anthropologists, accordingly, are by no means inclined to regard race mixture as a misfortune—at least not those anthropologists who study the question of interest to the human race by studying man himself and not the processes of the chicken-coop or the florist's hothouse.

In the lecture delivered by Luschan at the Racial Congress, which we have already quoted several times, this scholar also has the following to say on the question of mixed races:

"We all know that a certain admixture of blood has

227

always been of great advantage to a nation. England, France and Germany are equally distinguished for the variety of their racial elements. In the case of Italy we know that in ancient times and at the Renaissance, Northern "Barbarians" were the leaven in the great advance of art and civilisation; and even Slavonic immigration has not been without effect on this movement. The marvellous ancient civilisation of Crete, again, seems to have been not quite autochthonous. We know also that the ancient Babylonian civilisation sprang from a mixture of two quite different national and racial elements, and we find a nearly homogeneous population in most parts of Russia and in the interior of China associated with a somewhat low stage of evolution."

Luschan does indeed seem inclined to regard mixtures between whites and blacks with disfavour. But he states his case cautiously in the paragraph immediately following the above quotation:

"On the other hand, we are all more or less disposed to dislike and despise a mixture of Europeans with the greater part of foreign races. 'God created the white man and God created the black man, but the ——— created the mulatto', is a very well-known proverb. As a matter of fact, we are absolutely ignorant as to the moral and intellectual qualities of half-castes. It would be absurd to expect from the union of a good-for-nothing European with an equally good-for-nothing black woman, children that march on the heights of humanity, and we know of many

half-castes that are absolutely *sans reproche;* but we have
no good statistics of the qualities of half-castes in comparison with those of their parents." [9]

It is apparent that Luschan is very far removed from
any acceptance of the popular conception—so carelessly
proclaimed by Zollschan as a demonstrated truth—namely,
that mongrels reproduce only the defects and vices of their
progenitors and not also their virtues.

In the case of mongrels between white races, he maintains the precise opposite. As for the products of unions
between whites and coloured people he considers the matter
as not sufficiently proved. No writer assigns any reason
for a worsening of character by reason of such mixture.
Zollschan, like Chamberlain himself, admits that the half-
castes may often excel their parents in physical strength,
in beauty, and in natural intelligence. But both declare
that the *character* suffers by reason of the mixture. Why
this degrading of race should be expressed precisely in the
character and not in any other trait appears to be a
decision of fate, and one requiring no explanation.

It is interesting to note that the defects due to a mingling of races express themselves only in the domain in
which they are least likely to be checked up. Nothing is
more subjective by nature than our judgment of the character of another individual. His external traits, his
strength, his talent, are subject to objective measurement,
but the impression made upon me by his character depends

[9] *Anthropological View of Race* (see footnote, pp. 22, 23).

in large measure on whether my intercourse with him is of friendly or hostile nature. Any man whose reputation has been subjected to distortion by party hatred and party favour will present an uncertain image in the records of history.[10] The same individual will present quite different traits in the eyes of his friends from those seen by his enemies. One may be the tenderest and kindliest father to one's children and yet be a most ruthless usurer or slave-driver. On the other hand, any specific expression of another's character will produce quite a different impression on the onlooker, depending on whether the latter is fighting by his side or constitutes a menace to his life. Character may express itself only in one's relation with others; manifestations of character depend entirely on one's relations with others; likewise, the evaluation of these manifestations by third persons will depend on such relations also. In a word, far more than in bodily stature, or in the strength or ability of the individual, the social factor, the influence of the environment, will assume the foreground in the impression made by his character. The factor of heredity appears here to be most variable and most difficult to be isolated and recognised as such.

But if we make an effort to ascertain the social factors producing the result that half-castes between whites and blacks appear for the most part to be of bad character, we

10 "Von der Parteien Gunst und Hass verzerrt,
Schwankt sein Charakterbild in der Geschichte."
—Friedrich Schiller, Prologue to *Wallensteins Lager.*

shall not have far to seek. We need only to refer to the "bastards" produced in Europe by parents of the same race, who are distinguished from the other children in the same country merely by the fact that they have been so unfortunate as to lack all the economic and social support which society and the law grant to legitimate children.

Nor do we find that the half-castes in the colonies have been subjected to worse judgements than the illegitimate children of European parents of "pure" race:

"In every respect, physically, mentally and morally, they constitute on the whole a debilitated, more or less degraded group. The mere fact that they were produced in extra-conjugal, illegitimate relations, becomes in their case a powerful cause of disease and death, both before and after birth, and throughout their entire lives. In the total statistics of disease, as well as in the mortality statistics of any country, they furnish, year in and year out, a very considerable and—we might add—constantly increasing contingent, both in physical as well as in mental diseases, mental debility, suicide, not to mention crimes of all kinds. Far more frequently than other groups, as compared with their number, they fill our public institutions, beginning with the lying-in hospital and the orphan asylum, and ending with the hospitals, the prisons, and the morgue." [11]

Why should we not expect to find that the facts obtaining of these unhappy pariahs in our society are also applicable to the half-castes in the colonies, almost all of

[11] Österlen, *Medizinische Statistik,* p. 200.

whom are illegitimate children—frequently as a result of the laws, for Christian governments, which know no closer concern than the protection of marriage and the family, do indeed permit white men to take coloured women as concubines, but not to marry them, and to permit their children to enjoy a father's care?

It should not surprise us to find that the coloured bastards lead just as sorry a life as the white bastards, and this fact would by no means prove that their general backwardness was due to their being of mixed extraction and not to their social position. But we find as a rule that bastards of barbarous tribes have far more chances of success than the illegitimate children of civilisation, which again does not of course prove that half-castes between Europeans and coloured races are of better endowment than children produced by two European parents. But their inferiority has not at all been proved. Under favourable circumstances, such half-castes may even give evidence of considerable ability.

Thus, Ratzel, in his *Völkerkunde*, speaks with great respect of the *bastaards*, the offspring of a mixture of white and Hottentot blood, who—it is claimed—have raised the Hottentots to a higher level. Ratzel has the following to say on this subject:

"It is claimed, concerning the European half-castes, in South Africa as well as in India and in South America, that they possess the defects of both their parents, but none of their virtues. In all these regions so much of this statement is true, that the half-castes to be sure rarely unite *all* the favourable traits of the European father with *all* the virtues of the coloured mother. But this is due less to the mixture of blood than to the peculiar and hardly favourable breeding which these persons receive and must receive by reason of their situation between two widely separated races. It is self-evident that the care of their education falls to the mother, and that therefore the first impressions received by the young half-caste are obtained in the environment of the lower race. As he grows up, he may become conscious of the superiority inherent in him as a rule—as far as his mentality is concerned, and often even physically—as a result of his share of the lighter blood; but the race to which his father belongs will not accept him; it will regard him as a coloured man, in spite of the better qualities he may have inherited as a half-caste. He will therefore grow up, usually, to receive less education and culture than his capacities would require, and it is quite natural that he should not be able—under these circumstances—to make the best use of his gifts in every case. Superior to the coloured community in mental endowment, in energy, and often even in physical strength, or at least in the spirit and love of putting his strength to the test, he lacks the gift of contentedness with his lowly and oppressed situation and with the phlegmatic insensibility to privations of every kind which are characteristic of his coloured brothers." [12]

[12] Ratzel, *Völkerkunde,* pp. 115, 116.

233

In other words, the "worsening" of the character of the half-castes consists in their furnishing less convenient objects of exploitation, and in their being more inclined to rebel against their subjection than the "pure" coloured race. Quite worthy of note is the judgement formed by Sidney Olivier, who, for a number of years, was governor of Jamaica, where there exists a considerable population of half-castes. In 1891, this island had only 15,000 whites, 122,000 half-castes, and about 500,000 Negroes. Olivier has a very high opinion of the latter and expects much from their future development. But of course the whites are at present far superior to them. In this connection, the half-castes may be considered socially an element of great value:

"The offspring of such breeding, whether legitimate or illegitimate, is, from the point of view of efficiency, an acquisition to the community, and, under favourable conditions, an advance on the pure bred African. For, notwithstanding all that it may be possible to adduce in favour of that prejudice against the mixed race, of which I have spoken, and which I have myself fully shared, I am convinced that this class as it at present exists, is a valuable and indispensable part of any West Indian community, and that a colony of black, coloured, and whites has far more organic efficiency and far more promise in it than a colony of black and white alone. A community of white and black alone is in far greater danger of remaining, so far as the unofficial classes are concerned, a community of employers and serfs, concessionaires and tributaries, with, at best, a bureaucracy to keep the peace between them. The graded mixed class in Jamaica helps to make an organic whole of the community and saves it from this distinct cleavage.

"A very significant light is thrown on the psychology of colour prejudice in mixed communities by the fact that, in the whites, it is stronger against the coloured than against the blacks. I believe this is chiefly because the coloured intermediate class do form such a bridge as I have described, and undermine, or threaten to undermine, the economic and social ascendancy of the white, hitherto the dominant aristocracy of these communities. This jealousy or indignation is much more pungent than the alleged natural instinct of race-aversion." [13]

In spite of the favourable results of many a mixture of Negroes and whites, it is nevertheless easy to understand why investigators who are favourably disposed to the coloured race may condemn a mingling between white and coloured. But this may hardly be considered as due to the laws of heredity, but rather to considerations of ethical and æsthetic nature.

The aversion to such mixtures is an aversion to the relations between the sexes found in regions where an unmarried white master class has unlimited control, in the colonies, over disfranchised natives. Such unions in these

[13] Sidney Olivier, *White Capital and Coloured Labour*, London, 1906, pp. 37-39.

countries will not partake of the character of a free love-selection, but rather of that of prostitution or even violation of the women involved. Such violent forms of race mixture should surely be condemned, but they have nothing to do with the question of heredity.

And surely they cannot be invoked in a consideration of the question as to whether the Jews should be preserved as a pure race by artificial segregation and by an avoidance of all mixed marriages.

We have seen that the Jews are in no sense a pure race; we have seen that even mixtures between widely separated races may be of advantage; and finally we have seen that mixtures between related races are as a rule of great value. Why should it be precisely the Jewish half-castes that have so disastrous an effect? On the contrary, it might be maintained that no mixture between European populations is likely to produce better results than that between Jews and non-Jews. No stratum of the population has become more one-sidedly urban in character than the Jews, and in no other stratum has in-breeding under unfavourable hygienic conditions produced more unhappy results than among the Jews.

It is Zollschan's opinion that "in-breeding within a human community of ten or eleven million" has "no longer the slightest similarity with in-breeding within the limits of a small group of relatives." But it is not true that the entire Jewish community lives in a single segregated region and that marriages take place only within this region. Jews in Vilna hardly regard Jewesses in Morocco or Yemen as possible mates. It is quite possible that the result of such matings might be a desirable one. But in many regions the Jews constitute a very small community, and the result very frequently is marriages between relatives, where the situation is such as to render impossible marriages outside of this community.

It might be possible to speak, however, of another form of in-breeding besides that within the family. Blood-relationship alone appears to be not a dangerous factor in marriage. It becomes dangerous only by reason of the probability that the same pathological predispositions have been inherited by both husband and wife and may therefore be transmitted to their children in an exaggerated form. But *acquired* defects may have just as much influence on posterity as those that are *inherited*, if present in both parents. This identity of acquired defects will most likely be present in those cases in which both husband and wife, as well as their ancestors for several generations, have been living and working under the same conditions. In this connection, it would be necessary to call attention not only to in-breeding within the family, but also to a vocational or social in-breeding. The more pernicious and one-sided the common conditions of labour and life of the two groups of ancestors, the more dangerous will be in-breeding within the vocation, as far as posterity is concerned; the more necessary a mingling with members of other vocations or classes; the greater the necessity, therefore—of course—

237

of technical and social reforms for eliminating noxious and one-sided tendencies.

Darwin also believed that alterations in the conditions of life, as well as the crossing of individuals who have been subject to different conditions of life, are of advantage, unless the alteration to which the individuals are subjected be too great.

"Hence it seems that, on the one hand, slight changes in the conditions of life benefit all organic beings, and on the other hand, that slight crosses, that is, crosses between the males and females of the same species, which have been subjected to slightly different conditions, or which have slightly varied, give vigour and fertility to the offspring." [14]

The Jews have suffered most from a uniformity of their conditions of life, since they have in their ranks but a modicum of variety in vocation, and since they lack particularly the invigorating influence of new accessions of peasant blood. And precisely in those regions in which they live together in great numbers, and where—therefore—the danger of in-breeding between blood-relations is smaller, their conditions of life are the most monotonous and unfavourable, and the dangers of vocational and social in-breeding become greatest for them. No stratum of the population has more to gain by an admixture of non-Jewish—more or less peasant—blood, than the Jews.

[14] Charles Darwin, *The Origin of Species*, The Harvard Classics, New York, 1909, chap. ix, p. 318.

PURE RACES AND MIXED RACES

The Jews have therefore not the slightest reason to avoid, because of fear of their assimilation, the only path to salvation that is available to them: *an energetic participation in the class struggle of the proletariat.*

CHAPTER XII

THE LAST STAGES OF JUDAISM

ZIONISM is an untenable Utopia. On the other hand, liberalism is no longer capable—and perhaps not even desirous—of carrying out what it has neglected hitherto. Besides, its resources and its backing in the population are weakening. Wherever the liberals have not succeeded in bringing about a complete emancipation of the Jews—not merely a legal emancipation, but a real social equality of the Jews—it is certain that they will not be able to do so in the future.

The capitalist Jews are in all countries content with what has been attained. Though they may not have gotten as much as they wished, they at least have power enough, by reason of their wealth, to overcome slight inconveniences. This was true even in Czarist Russia, and in places where it is not the case these disabilities do not appear important enough, in their eyes, to justify a risk of revolution in order to overcome them. The capitalist Jews themselves are becoming conservative and are accepting conditions as they are.

The only force capable of a thorough overturning of the present order and of a complete destruction of all oppression, of all legal and social inequality, now remains the proletariat, which must achieve this end in order to achieve its own liberation. Only a victorious proletariat can bring complete emancipation for the Jews; all of Jewry, except in so far as it is already fettered to capitalism, is interested in a proletarian victory.

There is no doubt that the liberation of the Jews will be equivalent to their absorption to the extent to which this liberation is achieved.

The centre of gravity of the Jewish question now lies in the great areas of former Russia. If Russia achieves full civil equality for the Jews, and if the country becomes economically prosperous and develops growing industries, we shall not again encounter a Jewish migration to the west. But this will mean that the process of Jewish assimilation, already so far advanced in the past, but somewhat retarded within the last decades, will again set in. Even in England and America, the assimilation of the new strata of Russian Jews will proceed at a rapid pace. If the accessions from Russia cease to arrive, probably the second generation and surely the third generation of the Jews in the London East End and on the East Side of New York, will no longer understand Yiddish but will all speak English; they will no longer live in a single section of the city, closely congested in a few sweated industries that yield but slight opportunity to live, but will spread throughout the country and find the same opportunities as the rest of the population for earning a living in the most

241

varied occupations. And religion will probably have become a matter of indifference to these Jews; thus the last barrier to their assimilation will be removed.

This prophecy, which I already made before the war, is also confirmed by the observation of Zollschan as contained in his book printed in 1919:

"The second generation of the inhabitants in this country speak Yiddish only in their parental environment, and later generations speak it only in unusual cases. . . . The Yiddish theatre has already passed beyond its culmination. My questions as to the basic reasons for this condition always brought the answer that the second generation has entirely lost interest in it as well as in the language itself." [1]

In the Chinese quarter Zollschan even found two Russian Jewesses who had married Chinese!

The process of the disintegration of Judaism will proceed more slowly in Eastern Europe than in America. But even in Eastern Europe, the process must go on, in spite of the fact that the struggle for the emancipation of the Jews has at this moment led to the laying of greater emphasis on their Jewish traits.

Like other nations who have been ruled by a master class which prevented them from securing contact with modern civilisation, the Jews of Russia have also created a literature in their own language, which hitherto had had no literature, as soon as they began to develop an aspiration

[1] Zollschan, *Revision des jüdischen Nationalismus,* p. 14.

towards independence. There resulted the growth of a Yiddish literature, a Yiddish theatre, a Yiddish press, which in America includes great daily newspapers and periodicals, and had already attained large dimensions even in Russia when the war opened.

"The 'Yiddish' daily press, after having been in existence for ten years, exceeds the Polish press in circulation and in Russia is second in this respect only to the Russian press proper."[2]

The productions and resources of an active national life on the part of the Russian Jews will become progressively greater and stronger as long as the struggle for Jewish freedom advances. But that which we call the Jewish nation can achieve the victory only in order then to disappear.

The Jewish nation could maintain itself only by means of a living together of all the Jews in close contact with each other. But the callings to which the great mass of the Jews in Eastern Europe chiefly flock are not compatible in great measure with such a congestion of population. Persons engaged in these callings can prosper only when they are living among great numbers of persons engaged in other occupations, in which the non-Jewish population predominates. Precisely the compulsory congestion of population in a small space—which today still gives plausibility to the conception of a Jewish nationality—has also created the specific Jewish misery. With the disappearance of the

[2] Hersch, *Le Juif*, p. 9.

latter will come also the disappearance of the conditions for a Jewish nationality. The Jewish misery can disappear only under a political and social condition of Eastern Europe which will impel the Jews in those regions to speak the language of their environment, which means the beginning of this assimilation. The latter will be further stimulated by the fact that in an Eastern Europe which is politically free, the intellectual advancement of the entire population will become one of the most important tasks of the state. Judaism draws its strength—as a specific group, segregated from its environment—from anti-Semitism alone, from persecution. In the absence of the latter, it would have been absorbed long ago. Counter-revolution might imbue Judaism with a new lease of life; but counter-revolution can be nothing more than a temporary phenomenon. When the Jews shall have ceased to be persecuted and outlawed, the Jews themselves will cease to exist.

Have we any reason to deplore this prospect?

Our answer will of course depend on the point of view from which we judge the matter. But it seems to me that for the Jew himself the ghetto—which is the specific Jewish form of life—is not a phenomenon calculated to give rise to melancholy longings. And the friends of human progress have far less cause than the conservative Jew to shed a tear over the disappearance of Judaism.

We have seen that Judaism developed to the highest point the properties of the city-dweller. These are precisely the mental properties at present most required for the progress of humanity. We find accordingly that the comparatively insignificant number of Jews in Western Europe has produced an astonishingly long list of epoch-making minds, the proud enumeration of which would extend from Baruch Spinoza to Heinrich Heine, Ferdinand Lassalle, and Karl Marx.

But although the Jews developed as their culminating properties such immense mental abilities, they became more and more unfitted to apply the abilities they had developed. Until late in the Middle Ages, the Jews, like the Catholic Church, had constituted an element of progress; but—again like the Catholic Church—they have since cut themselves off from progress; even more than the Catholic Church, owing to the narrow limits of Judaism and its strict segregation from the non-Jewish world, which had begun to widen its horizon immensely after the Fifteenth Century, and to pass through an era of continuous mental revolutions, the Jewish community ceased to participate in the work of progress. The Jews, restricted to the ghetto by their orthodoxy, remained totally untouched by this great transformation of the human mind; they assumed a hostile position to the new philosophy. The spiritual giants produced by modern Judaism could bring their forces into action only after they had burst the fetters of Judaism. Their activities were carried on, without exception, outside of the bounds of Judaism, and within the realm of modern culture, which is as little Jewish as it is Christian, and often their activities were in complete conscious opposition to Judaism—by which we mean, as it may be necessary to point out again, not the total number of Jews, but those Jews who are comprised in a specific group and as such are cut off from the rest of mankind. Even the pioneers of Zionism, such men as Herzl, Nordau, Zangwill, make use of the so-called world languages and not of "Yiddish". The Jews have become an eminently revolutionary factor, while Judaism has become a reactionary factor. It is like a weight of lead attached to the feet of the Jews who eagerly seek to progress, one of the last remnants of the feudal Middle Ages, a social ghetto still maintaining its existence in the consciousness, after the tangible, physical ghetto has disappeared. We cannot say we have completely emerged from the Middle Ages as long as Judaism still exists among us. The sooner it disappears, the better it will be, not only for society, but also for the Jews themselves.

The disappearance of the Jews will not involve a tragic process like the disappearance of the American Indians or the Tasmanians. It will not be equivalent to a declining into stupidity and degradation, but to a rising to greater strength, to prosperity and well-being, to the opening up of an immense field of activity. It will not mean a mere shifting of domicile from one mediæval ruin to another, not a transition from orthodox Judaism to ecclesiastical Christianity, but the creation of a new and higher type of man.

THE LAST STAGES OF JUDAISM

Ahasuerus, the Wandering Jew, will at last have found a haven of rest. He will continue to live in the memory of man as man's greatest sufferer, as he who has been dealt with most severely by mankind, to whom he has given most.

INDEX

A

Abraham, eponymic hero, 73
Adultery, 61
Afghanistan, 71
Africa, 36, 68, 91, 92, 166, 184, 232
Agassiz, Jean Louis Rodolphe, 64
Agriculture, Jewish, 188–192, 194–198
Ahasuerus, King, 177, 247
Alaska, 52
Alcoholism, 131–133, 226
Alexandria, 113, 136, 138, 184
Algeria, 94
America, 165, 166, 232
Ammon, Otto, 15, 16
Amorites, 220
Amsterdam, Holland, 154
Ancona sheep, 24
Andrée, Richard, 90
Anglo-Saxons, 66
Animals, *see* Domestic Animals, Wild Animals
Antelopes, survival of, 36
Anthropology, *passim*
Anthropo-sociologists, 20
Anthropozoon biblicum, 71
Anti-Semitism, *passim*
Anti-vaccinationists, *see* Vaccination
Apes, *see* Monkeys
Aquiline nose, *see* Nose
Arabia, 108, 109, 212
Arabs, the, 12, 68, 134, 140, 191, 206, 210, 211

Argentina, 177
Armenians, the, 73, 108
Armenoids, the, 73, 108, 109, 127
Artificial selection, 27, 28, 139
Aryans, the, 15, 66, 86, 103, 125
Ashkenazim, 191
Asia, 71–74, 82, 91, 207, 211, 212
Assyrian monuments, 27
Auerbach, physician, 101
Austria, 152, 154, 160, 172, 175, *footnote,* 210
Australia, 71, 72
Avignon, France, 147

B

Babylon, ancient city, 184
Babylonia, 210, 228
Babylonian Exile, 185
Baden, German province, 15, 16
Ballod, Professor Karl, 195–198, 210
Barbary lion, 32
Bavaria, 92, 93, 107
Belgium, 171
Beluchistan, 71
Berlin, Germany, 99, 100, 153, 172, 177
Berliner Tageblatt, 195
Bernard, Samuel, 123
Biology, 19
Bismarck, Prince, 68
Blond type, 93, 94
Blumenbach, Johann Friedrich, 64, 90
Boas, Franz, 42
Body plasm, 37, 39

249

INDEX

250

INDEX

Denmark, 155, 156
Desmoulins, Charles, 64, 65
Diabetes, 101, 102
Diaspora, 184
Diseases, "Jewish," 101–103, 226
Dolichocephalic, 15, 95
Domestic animals, 20–25, 60, 222–226
Driesmans, Heinrich, 15

E

Egeberth, Jew of Cologne, 146
Egypt, 110, 112, 211, 212
Egyptian monuments, 27
Elbe, river, 120
Employment, in Palestine, 200, 201
Engels, Friedrich, 123
England, 86, 107, 117, 154, 157, 171, 173, 175, 184, 211, 212, 228
Environment, effect of, 42, 43, 46, 47, 49
Eskimos, 121
Esther, 177
Evolution, 18, 27, 28, 50, 76
Eyes, colour of, 40, 65, 93

F

Farmers, *see* Agriculture
Fecundity of the Jews, 98–100
Fellahs, 210
Fidelity of wives, 61, 118
Finns, 175
Fischer, Kuno, 139, *footnote*
Fishberg, Maurice, 18, 42, 90–96, 98, 99, 104, 127
Forster, George, 58
Foundations of Christianity, by Karl Kautsky, 113–115, 117, 137, 138
Foundations of the Nineteenth Century, *see* Chamberlain, Houston Stuart

Fox-terriers, 225
France, 86, 99, 121–123, 154, 160, 171, 173, 193, 211, 214, 228
Frankfort-on-the-Main, 153
Freemasonry, 115
French, the, 175
French Revolution, 15, 151, 214
Freytag, Gustav, 105

G

Galicia, Poland, 152
Garment industries, Jews in, 167
Geology, 31
Germ plasm, 87, 39
German language, *see* Yiddish, *and* Wagner, Richard
Germanic race, *see* Teutonic race
Germany, 99, 100, 102, 103, 107, 152–154, 160, 165, 171, 172, 175, 193, 196, 197, 210, 228
Ghetto, the, 117, 118, 144, 149, 156, 217–245, 246
Gibraltar, 72
Gobineau, Comte Joseph Arthur de, 220
Goethe, Johann Wolfgang von, 211, *footnote*
Gorilla, 70
Gotha, German city, 42
Grapes, in Palestine, 197
Graubünden, 74
Great Britain, 165
Greek language, 65, 66, 68, 69, 113
Guttmann, Julius, 123
Guzerat lion, 32

H

Häckel, Ernst, 65, 76
Hair, color of, 40, 65, 93, 120
Haman, Imperial chancellor, 177
Hamburg, Germany, 154

251

INDEX

252

INDEX

INDEX

254

INDEX

255

INDEX